# THE SPIRIT ENSHRINED

Meditations on

## MARY, SPOUSE OF THE HOLY GHOST

BY

### ANTHONY PATTISON, O.F.M.Cap.

NEW YORK CITY
JOSEPH F. WAGNER, INC.
LONDON: B. HERDER

Nihil Obstat ex parte Ordinis:
EDWINUS FAVIER, O.F.M.Cap., S.T.D.
*Censor deputatus*

Imprimi Potest:
THOMAS NOLAN, O.F.M.Cap.
*Minister Provincial*

Nihil Obstat:
JOHN M. A. FEARNS, S.T.D.
*Censor Librorum*

Imprimatur:
✠ FRANCIS CARDINAL SPELLMAN, D.D.
*Archbishop of New York*

AUTHOR'S NOTE

These meditations owe their origin to a course of talks given to the parishioners of the Capuchin Priory Church, Oxford, England, for the May devotions, 1938. Most of the New Testament quotations are from the Confraternity edition; all other Scripture quotations are taken from the Douay version.

# DEDICATION

To

FATHER JOHN MARY

(Co-founder of the Pious Union of the Holy Ghost)

of the

English Province of Capuchin Friars Minor,

who in his life and work

inspired so many with the love he had

of the

Divine Spirit, and Mary, His Spiritual Vessel,

these thoughts are humbly dedicated.

*Rev. Leopold J. Czeky, S.J*

# Foreword

In days of doubt and indecision, when men seek a solution to national and international problems, and think only of man-made plans, it is well if we turn to the Sacred Scriptures, there to rediscover the plan of life as offered to us by Christ our Savior. In the Gospel of St. John we read: "But the Paraclete, the Holy Ghost, whom the Father will send in my name, he will teach you all things and bring all things to your mind, whatsoever I shall have said to you" (John, xiv. 26). The teachings of Christ constitute the plan of life for mankind. Unfortunately, mankind has either rejected, neglected or forgotten that plan. To-day, as of old, we need the Holy Spirit to teach us all things and to bring back to the mind of the world all things whatsoever Christ has taught; for it will only be when all things *are* "restored in Christ" that we may hope for peace and tranquillity once more.

The work of the Holy Spirit in the soul of man is something to which insufficient attention is paid; and in the present series of meditations, offered to us by the Reverend Father Anthony Pattison, O.F.M. Cap., the author shows the working of the Holy Spirit in her who was His Spouse, the Virgin Mother of God. Skilfully and clearly, the author draws for us a pen picture of Mary under the influence of God the Holy Ghost. We see a gradual unfolding of a life lived in complete accord with the will of God. We see her who was destined to be the Mother of mankind, gradually being molded and formed under the influence of the Holy Spirit to play the great rôle to which she had been called.

Not only do these meditations provide us with an insight into the life of Our Lady, not only do we see the workings of the Holy Spirit within her, but they also provide us with some very practical lessons and principles to be learned and applied in our own daily lives. Only as we allow the Holy Spirit of God to enter into our souls, to teach us all things and bring back to our minds all things that Our Lord taught, can we ever hope to make our way out of the gloom into the light. Only in so far as we coöperate with the Holy Spirit of God, only as we allow Him to form and mold us, can we ever hope to "renew the face of the earth" (Ps., ciii. 30).

# Contents

# CONTENTS

# Re-Awakenings

*Thou shalt send forth thy spirit, and they shall be
created; and thou shalt renew the face of the earth
(Ps., ciii. 30).*

Catholic tradition and devotion have always associated the Holy Spirit of God and the Virgin
Mother of Jesus with springtide. The month of
April is dedicated to devotion to the Holy Ghost,
that of May to Mary. Often enough in the liturgical calendar the great Feast of Pentecost, the com-
memoration of the coming of the Spirit of God
and May devotions to Mary combine to make this
association the more marked.

The analogy between what, as creatures, we owe
to the return of spring, and what, as children of
God, we owe to the Holy Spirit and the Mother of
God, is an obvious one. Cardinal Newman used
this analogy with classic effect in that great sermon
of his, "The Second Spring," recording the return
of England to the Catholic Faith; and, in that same

sermon, he linked together the names of the Paraclete and Mary, as it seemed to him that the revival
of faith which he saw in that land owed most to
devotion to the Spirit, and to the constant prayer
of the Mother of God.

The Holy Spirit of God is the breath of God's
life; where He breathes, new life springs forth
from that which was falling into corruption, because from Him came forth all things living: "And
the earth was void and empty, and darkness was
upon the face of the deep. And the Spirit of God
moved over the waters" (Gen., i. 2). So it was in
the beginning, and so it will be till the end. Every
new manifestation of life which has reference to
God, whether in individuals or in organizations,
has its origin in the vivifying power of the Holy
Ghost.

Springtide, the month of April in particular, is
dedicated to devotion to the Holy Spirit. But Holy
Mother Church did not intend our devotion to stop
there. This devotion was meant to be fruitful
throughout the year. Devotion to the Holy Spirit
in the Spring was meant to prepare us for the glories of May.

Devotion to the Mother of God finds its climax in the Month of May, because it is impossible to think of Mary without associating her with the rebirth of our whole supernatural life, when she gave unto us the Word of God, our Savior. From that moment the winter-darkness of paganism saw a new light breaking upon the world; it was the "Light of the gentiles," Jesus Christ the Son of God. The glories of Mary, which we commemorate in May, bring to life again the great mysteries of our new life in God; they recall the constant intervention of the Mother of God in the life of the Mystical Body of Her Son when, in the dark hours of the history of the Church, she has brought the allegiance of men back again to the service of God, and reawakened the primitive charity of the early Church.

The difficulty which most of the faithful meet in their devotion to the Holy Spirit (and without this there can be no great revival of Catholic life in the world) can be overcome by an indirect approach to the Holy Spirit. We must seek Him in the works of His hands, in those things which He has sanctified, in those whom He has filled with the breath of His life.

The following considerations are almost wholly concerned with the Mother of God, who in a unique manner enshrined the Spirit of God. When we meditate upon the interior spirituality of the Virgin Mary, we are looking upon the intimate operation of the Holy Ghost within the soul, and seeing how His Gifts found their greatest perfection. When we meditate upon Mary and her close association with the Mysteries of the Incarnation, the Joyful and Glorious Mysteries of the Holy Rosary, we are at the same time focusing our attention upon how those virtues, given to the Mother of God by the Holy Spirit, found expression in her external contacts with men, and how, guided by the Spirit of God, she met the particular situations, each of which had a place and purpose in the designs of God. When we meditate upon the Mother of Jesus in the Mysteries of the Mystical Body, we are concerned at the same time with the work of the Paraclete who was sent to guide and vivify the Church of Christ.

This approach to the Sanctifier of souls, through

4

meditation upon the figure of the Holy Virgin, should bring us much closer to the Spirit of Truth; it should make us realize how His holy operation must be vital in our own lives; it should awaken within us a desire to make the Holy Spirit better known and better loved by others, while at the same time we enrich our souls by His holy graces and loving influence.

## II

# Vision of Eternal Things

*I will espouse thee to me in faith; and thou shalt know that I am the Lord (Osee, ii. 20).*

To most of us the gift of faith is so much a part of our lives that it is almost impossible for us to realize what life would be without it. Perhaps only those who have lived for many years deprived of this gift can make a real comparison between life's values with and without this power of believing in the realities beyond our senses and human understanding.

Of the three great gifts given to us in Baptism, faith is the most basic. We may lose charity, we may be deprived of hope, yet faith may remain; and as long as it remains, there is always the possibility that hope and charity will return. Our hope is bound up in the light of faith. As long as that flame is alive, however faint it may be, there is always the possibility that it will reënkindle our

6

desire for the supernatural. Our supernatural charity is based upon our knowledge, for we cannot
love that which we do not know, and all our supernatural knowledge comes through the gift of divine
love called faith.

The assent of faith, that first conscious act of the
will, by which we believe without doubting in the
revealed truths of God, is the most tremendous act
of our lives. By it the Holy Ghost leads us into a
world unknown and unrealized by the man and
woman from whom this gift is withheld. Having
made that assent, that recognition of the supernatural life, a man will never again be the same. He
will always continue to be something better, something greater, than he was before. Or, on the contrary, he will continue to be something worse,
something more miserable, if he has been unfaithful
to this gift of the Holy Spirit. For a pearl of great
price has been placed within his hands; the key to
the secrets of a life hidden with his God has been
given to him; the threshold of a new world has
been opened to him. He must either take these
occasions and walk forward to greater and greater
new discoveries, or go back among those who have

never been given a glimpse of this other-world, and there he must forever be frustrated by the realization of the narrowness of the world he has chosen, the pettiness of its purposes, and the shallowness of its pleasures. There will always be with him the realization of the fact of that "other-world"; for, by faith once received, he has seen it, and, by being unfaithful to it, he is as a blind man living now by senses which can never take the place of sight.

The faithfulness of Mary must not be considered merely in that aspect which we may term "being true" to God, or being faithful to her great vocation. Rather should we consider the fullness of her faith, if we would rightly understand her whom we call the Virgin Most Faithful. It is not enough for us to say that the Holy Ghost declared her "full of grace" and, therefore, full of faith.

This gift of faith was within Mary from the moment of her conception. We know nothing for certain of the workings of the Holy Ghost through this gift until the moment of the Annunciation. Then, so tremendous is this occasion, so breath-taking this event, that we realize how full of faith the Virgin of Nazareth must have been to exclaim:

"Be it done to me according to thy word" (Luke, i. 38). "And the Word was made flesh and dwelt among us" (John, i. 14). The life of faith she had lived before must, indeed, have been deep for her to assent with this simplicity. Zachary needs a sign to make him believe that he will be the father of a son born out of due time; Mary asks no sign when she is to be the Mother of the Son of God! She only asks whether this invitation of the angel is compatible with her virginity; given that, her assent of faith is full and unconditioned.

The measure of supernatural faith is the number and nature of the difficulties placed in the way of *continued assent* to the will of God. It is thus that, in our human way, we measure the sanctity of the men and women throughout all ages who have followed the path of faith: the martyrs, the confessors and virgins of the Mystical Body of Christ.

We have no reason to suppose that the Virgin of Nazareth had a full revelation as to *all* that would follow upon the assent of faith given by her at the Annunciation. In those few places where we have a picture of the Virgin Mother, we should be led to conclude that the future was only partially known to her; indeed, that the present events of her motherhood were often perplexing to her: "Son, why hast thou done so to us?" (Luke, ii. 48).

It would seem true to say that her very office of motherhood brought with it an overwhelming need of faith. The Holy Spirit of God, as we have already suggested, led her by the gradual path of faith; but it was a path neither straight nor even; it never gave her a clear view of what was to come, except that at certain stages in the journey she saw the outline of a gibbet—the Cross. Once, for three long days, her Divine Son was lost from that path along which the Holy Spirit was leading her; for three years His way was to be very different from her own. When their ways did again converge, she was to find Him on the *Via Dolorosa,* and to follow to the grave the Body which she had carried within her.

Can we measure the faith that never faltered during those years? Can we wonder that the Holy Spirit of God had a reward, beyond all rewards, for a faith that could see His will in all the circumstances of that life at Nazareth and the years that followed? For it is by the fact that Mary ever lived in the reality of her faith that she lives now in the minds and hearts of men and women, separated from her time by centuries, but united to her in their fellowship with her Son. It is by her fidelity that she has become the mother of men, and all generations shall call her blessed. It is truly thus that she has become the Virgin Most Faithful; and faith itself has given way to that fullness of the vision of God, whom she knew, loved and served as His handmaid; to the vision of that God whom she gave to us in the Person of the Word, and to the love of that Spirit by whom she was overshadowed and whom she so fully enshrined.

# III

## *Expectation*

*The God of hope fill you with all joy and peace in believing; that you may abound in hope and in the Holy Spirit (Rom., xv. 13).*

One of the most treasured and beautiful virtues of the Christian religion, and one which is, perhaps, all too readily taken for granted, is the virtue of hope.

Of faith St. Paul says it "is the substance of things to be hoped for, the evidence of things that are not seen" (Heb., xi. 1). By the seeds sown in our hearts by the Holy Spirit at Baptism, the Christian soul reaches out to things beyond the present; it becomes hungry for those things which give permanence, which will fully satisfy unto true happiness. "Our hearts, O Lord, are restless till they rest in Thee," writes St. Augustine in his *Confessions.*

The degree of faith enkindled by the Holy Spirit of Love gives solidity to our hope. This is what St.

Paul means when he speaks of faith giving "substance to our hopes." Hope, the supernatural virtue, is not a vain desire for the unattainable. Faith feeds our hope with the truths and mysteries beyond unaided human reason. They are truths guaranteed by the infinite wisdom and knowledge of God. In so far as these truths concern the future of the human soul, they are also guaranteed by the infinite power and mercy of God, and by the essential integrity of God, who will fulfill what He has promised.

It is through faith, then, that our hope is a solid and unshakable conviction. It gives all sturdiness to religious effort; it gives a firm ground for us to persevere in the presence of what might daunt us, in the presence of what is obscure; it enables a man to go forward in the presence of a darkness and human uncertainty which would be a natural impediment to any further effort or achievement.

The virtue of hope has been vigorously attacked by the materialism of the age. Materialism is, of its nature, bound up with the present. It can advance only step by step, as the means are provided by nature itself. Materialism gives only a very limited form of hope, in the sense that any future good which may be desired, or foreseen, is already bound up in present achievement. It can see these "hopes" only in the obscurity of present scientific research and trial by error. Many of the promises of science and materialism are more than half nullified by the evident evils inherent in an imperfect mode of life. The many good things promised and hoped for by atomic science are almost entirely done away with by the overwhelming fear that the very same science may bring to millions of others, as it did to hundreds of thousands, destruction, injury and loss of the means of life.

In this sense materialism can never give hope to humanity, for it is the slave of the present. In this sense also materialism is consequently a way of despair, for despair is the absence of hope.

Our hope is in the fact that it is the Holy Spirit who brings the breath of a new life. "Send forth thy Spirit, and they shall be created, and thou shalt renew the face of the earth" (Ps., ciii. 30). Renew it in hope.

It is not surprising that Christian hope is a folly to those who live only for the present. The denial of God throws man back upon his own resources. This limits him to his own narrow experience; his future becomes uncertain; any idea of life hereafter is lost to him, because he has denied the very reason for human immortality, God Eternal.

Christian hope is a personal gift; it does not merely promise something for the future of the human race. It rests upon the infallible revelation of God, upon the omnipotence of His will, upon the providence of the Eternal Father. Linked with hope is the gift of holy fear (which we will consider more fully in another place). Our hope rests upon God, but we are also aware that its fulfillment rests partly upon our own achievement: to live in the charity of God, to remain united with Him by grace.

The basic mystery upon which the supernatural hope of the Christian man is founded and, indeed, upon which the true hope of the world is grounded, is the mystery of the Incarnation.

When the Divine Spirit of God overshadowed the Virgin of Nazareth, a twofold promise was given to man. In the first place, the "promise of ages" had been fulfilled; the hope of the nations was no longer something of the future, it was a reality: "The Word was made flesh and dwelt among us" (John, i. 14). But the very purpose of His presence in the flesh was to manifest to us the greater promise of the future. Our eternal hope rests upon the fulfillment of the promise made to our fathers (Luke, i. 55), having been fulfilled by the overshadowing of the Virgin Mary by the Spirit of God.

To Mary, by the power of the Holy Ghost, it was given to be the instrument both of the fulfillment of God's promise and of the hope of the Redeemer, and to be the one to bring forth the hope of the world to come.

For this reason has she been given the titles, "Ark of the Covenant" and "Gate of Heaven." Christian tradition has given to the Mother of God a very special place as advocate on our behalf, because she was so closely associated with every phase and event of the mystery which so intimately concerns our future.

We have considered the Mother of God in the light of the gift of faith. According to the measure of her faith we can rightly understand the extent of her hope. Her words, "behold henceforth all

16

generations shall call me blessed" (Luke, i. 48), are anchored in her realization of God's power to fulfill: ". . . mindful of his mercy, even as he spoke to our fathers" (Luke, i. 54-55).

There is a beautiful prayer offered to Mary, one which rises from the hearts of men and women surrounded by the uncertainties of a materialistic world. It is a prayer to Mary the Star of the Sea, that *her* hope, now a fulfillment in heaven, may shine upon us and this world which has forgotten to hope in the ever powerful Spirit of God . . . "May her sweet name be lisped by little ones, and linger on the lips of the aged and dying; may it be invoked by the hopeful and hymned by the joyful, that this Star of the Sea being their protection and their guide, all may come to the harbor of eternal salvation" (Prayer for the Conversion of England).

IV

# So This is Love

*Her ways are beautiful ways, and all her paths are peaceable (Prov., iii. 17).*

Even a cursory reading of St. Paul's First Letter to the Corinthians will convince us of the diversity of the characteristics of the virtue of charity. It is the living principle, the source of life in the spiritual sphere, just as the soul of man is the principle of life in the body. Hence, we must expect to find charity accountable for every action which merits a supernatural reward.

When we are considering charity as the virtue infused into the soul by the Holy Spirit of God at Baptism, we are considering charity in a very particular way. To be technical for a moment, we are considering charity as a cause of life, not its effects. Our manner of speech, our manifestations of love and hate, our achievements of brain and brawn—all these we clumsily call life, when we mean the effects of life being within us. So, we name all the good works we do as charity—which "is patient, is kind, feels no envy, is never perverse or proud, sustains, believes, hopes, endures"—when we are really referring to the effects of charity. In the same chapter xiii, St. Paul shows how we may manifest many of these effects: "If I have all faith . . . And if I distribute all my goods to feed the poor, and if I deliver my body to be burned, yet do not have charity, it profits me nothing." If the *cause* of all meritorious work is absent, the overflow of effects is of no avail.

The gift of the virtue of charity is, then, supernatural. It is a power added to our *natural* goodness; it is a source of a new kind of life—one which may live or die within us. The comparison which St. Paul draws for us, shows how real it is. We may *do* things which look very like charity (giving all our goods to the poor), but if the virtue, the power of the Holy Ghost, is not *really* present within us, it is only a counterfeit charity, of no value in the supernatural life.

The power of the Holy Ghost is the core of our supernatural life. The virtue of charity, is man's share in the divine nature (II Pet., i. 4), and participation in the life of the Person of Divine Love, the Holy Spirit.

When the virtue of faith has fallen from us, as it will when we see God face to face; when the virtue of hope is no longer present, for it will no longer be ours to hope when we possess God for all eternity; when this transformation takes place, the virtue of charity will remain. True, it also will be transformed into eternal union with God, but in essence, of its nature, it will remain the same.

It is not faith, it is not hope, but it is charity which makes us the adopted sons of God. It is the Father who calls us to be His sons: "No one can come to Me except the Father draw him" (John, vi. 44). It is *through* the Word of God that we become His co-heirs: "I am the Way, the Truth and the Life" (John, xiv. 6). It is *by* the Spirit of God that we are elevated and transformed into this sonship. "Unless a man be born again of water and the Spirit, he cannot enter into the Kingdom of God" (John, iii. 5).

All the works of the Holy Ghost, and we shall see how manifold they are, are centered upon this virtue of charity, given to us when we are "born not of blood, nor of the will of the flesh, nor of the will of man, but of God" (John, i. 13). All the Gifts of the Spirit of Love are given to us to enlighten or strengthen this new life of charity born in the womb of our human nature, until such a time as we shall have so accomplished the work of the Spirit that we may bring forth the image of the Son of God unto eternity.

In his Epistle to the Romans, St. Paul speaks of us being grafted onto a new branch, where we shall find a new life in Christ. This work of the Holy Spirit, through His gifts and graces, is very significant. It means that we retain much of the natural appearances of life with our own fellowmen, but that all of those appearances are changed by the character of the life which is in them, for it is the life of the Vine, which is Christ. "The branch cannot bear fruit of itself unless it remain on the vine . . . He who abides in me, and I in him, he bears much fruit" (John, xv. 4-5).

The virtue of charity imparted to us by the Holy Spirit finds so many manifestations because of the variety of its fruits in all of those who are grafted to the Vine, which is Christ. It is both one and multiple—one in its source, the Holy Spirit of Love, and multiple in its works.

The mark by which we are known as the disciples of Christ does not come directly from the sign of faith, nor yet from the hope we have through faith in His promises; it comes directly from the virtue of charity: "By this will all men know that you are my disciples, if you have love for one another" (John, xiii. 35). We may have faith and hope, and yet be wanting in the chief characteristic of a Christian.

This bond of charity with the Holy Spirit of Love belongs to no special vocation, to no particular section of the Mystical Body of Christ. It has made those whom we call Saints, and we find them in every walk of life. It is by this bond of charity that we are one with all of those who share in the glory of the Church Triumphant: for they have no longer need of faith and hope, but possess the fullness of the charity of Christ.

Though so powerful and multiple in its effects, charity is a lowly virtue; it finds a place in the most humdrum and routine affairs of daily life. It is just precisely in this aspect that we can take encouragement from the life of the Mother of God.

Though Mary was sanctified in a special way by the Holy Ghost, in view of her office as the Mother of God, yet she did have her "own spiritual life," and it was very much "hidden in God." And this life of hers, as an individual, was made glorious in the eyes of the angels, because all her words, thoughts and actions were bound together by the virtue of charity. The fact that the Angel Gabriel greets her with a new title, "full of grace," even before she has heard of or accepted the vocation of the Divine Maternity, gives us the key to the fullness of her sanctity; and we have seen that there can be no sanctity without the virtue of charity. To ask oneself honestly and frankly what were the opportunities of holiness given to Mary of Nazareth, before she became the Mother of God, is to answer a searching question concerning ourselves. If Mary was full of grace at the moment of the Annunciation, it was because the very limited sphere of life in which she lived, made her concentrate upon turning everything into a tribute to the love of God. Charity pervaded her domestic life;

it enriched her thoughts; it gave motive to the most insignificant of her neighborly actions; it made her content with her lowly lot and without envy for those in a better position. Charity is a very economical virtue, and so it was with Mary: it gathered up the fragments of her life, lest they be lost.

The inspiration given to thousands of men and women throughout the world, and in every generation (in particular to nuns like the Little Sisters of the Poor), all comes from the charity of the Lowly Maid of Nazareth, who enshrined within herself the Holy Spirit of Love, and made glorious in her domestic life the virtues of faith, hope and charity, the foundation of our union with the Holy Ghost, and concerning which Scripture says: "The greatest of these is charity" (I Cor., xiii. 13).

# V

## *Harmony*

*With the bread of life and understanding she shall feed him (Ecclus., xv. 3).*

We have seen something of the importance of the first assent of faith—the "fiat" of the Holy Spirit in bringing a light of revelation into our darkness, our "fiat" in stepping forward voluntarily into this new world of the supernatural, a world like a new creation, for such it truly is.

This, however, is only a beginning of the Holy Spirit's operation in our soul. When God created our universe, He did not leave His work to continue, except by His all-necessary sustaining power. When He reveals Himself supernaturally to man by faith, He does not leave him without the means of finding Him in the brightness of the light of faith.

The Holy Spirit gives to man the supernatural gift and power of penetrating the meaning of his faith. This is not done by reasoning and thought, though these have their part to play. It is rather by a gift of focusing our mind upon this new world of experience discovered by faith. It is a power of harmonizing *our* position as men and creatures of God with *His* supernatural end and purpose in life, and for eternity.

We are like men who look into a new world through some powerful instrument; but that instrument must be adjusted to our own particular gift of sight. In order that the details may become real to us, we must adjust it this way and that, until we have an exact vision of all that lies ahead of us, and we can see whither we are going. And we see it in a particular and personal way. It is through the instrumentality of the gift of the Holy Ghost, the personal Gift of Understanding, that this adjustment of our personal faith is made.

Though the Mother of God was given the gift of faith in a way and for a purpose unique among men, it was only through the Gift of Understanding that the particular events of her adventure of faith became harmonized in her mind, and gave to her that tranquillity of soul so characteristic of her.

We have noted the tremendous gift of faith which caused her to assent to the overshadowing of the Holy Spirit. A clear instance of the operation of the Holy Ghost through His Gift of Understanding was that Mary could harmonize this great office of Divine Motherhood with her virginity. Here was mystery indeed! Her acceptation of this mystery was not by reasoning; the harmony of what seemed so contradictory was made, and could only be made, by the operation of the Holy Spirit, through the supernatural Gift of Understanding. There was, no longer, doubt about this *circumstance* of her vocation; there was instant and spontaneous acceptance of the fact as declared by the messenger. Faith and Understanding worked together under the power of the Gift of the Holy Spirit.

It was thus that, through this particular gift, the Virgin harmonized all the uneven and seemingly contradictory events of her life of faith.

Thus, the poverty she had to offer her Child at Bethlehem came to be harmonized with the riches and worship of the Magi. She accepted, if not then fully penetrating, the mystery of the sword which was to pierce her soul; just as she accepted, at the same time, the joy of the Presentation. Mary was the first to ask her Son to use His divine power in an act of charity at a marriage feast; it was her "understanding" faith which could penetrate His seeming reluctance to work a miracle at that time. Need we speak of those deeper mysteries of His Passion and Death which she was to reconcile with His Divinity?

Even though we see this Gift of Understanding working within the faith-life of Mary in such a sublime manner, we must not consider it working only in the higher levels of sanctity. We must not think of it as some kind of spiritual luxury given only to choice souls.

On the contrary, it is an essential instrument of the Holy Ghost given to every man and woman who would walk in the supernatural path of faith. Indeed, we may say that it would be dangerous in the extreme to attempt to walk by faith without the use of this Gift. Just as it would be dangerous for a shortsighted man to walk abroad without his spectacles.

Our purpose in life, no less than that of the Virgin Mother's, is to know, love and serve God. It is impossible to follow her in this knowledge, love and service, unless the Holy Spirit of God works through and within us by the use of this Gift of Understanding. Faith may show us our supernatural purpose, but how are we to penetrate the mystery of knowing God, of loving Him, and learn in what things we are to serve Him?

On the lowest rung of the ladder of perfection, Understanding will teach us what things we are to avoid; on the second rung, we shall penetrate something of the perfection of our Maker—and our own imperfection, our need of following the counsels of Christ; on the highest rungs, it is only through this Gift that we can truly contemplate "with all the saints, what is the breadth, and length, and height, and depth, and to know Chirst's love which surpasses knowledge, in order that you may be filled unto all the fullness of God" (Eph., iii. 18).

# VI

## *Spiritual Poise*

*I directed my soul to her and in knowledge I found her (Ecclus., li. 27).*

In our effort to discover for ourselves the personality of some historic character, often enough, we are most deeply affected by some trait which is all too difficult to define. It is a certain power of mind and will to meet exceptional events in a manner which makes the man or woman stand out above others.

The very fact that a certain person still lives in the minds of men, causes us to take for granted many of his characteristics which made him outstanding among his contemporaries.

The qualities of mind and body which make a great discoverer famous in his own day are, most often, summed up in the words: self-confidence, vision, courage, tenacity of purpose, organizing ability, fortitude in the face of difficulties. These have carried him above the heads of his fellows; they have carried him forward into posterity. When we try to rediscover his personality by research, we take these characteristics for granted, we list them, perhaps underline, them; but, what is of more interest to us, is discovering other human traits which make him one with ourselves, though he be so different. His courage we take for granted; his kindliness and consideration for others who shared his adventures is a new, a surprising and pleasant feature we have not before recognized. It is these unexpected, yet revealing, characteristics which make biography so appealing, even in the case of those whose lives have been written and rewritten many times.

The lives of the Saints have this in common with secular biographies, that their lives are no less intriguing than those of men and women who have won fame in other spheres of life. In the lives of the Saints we are dealing with new and powerful influences which are much less capable of definition. We are dealing with the influences of the Divine Sanctifier, "whose ways are not our ways." In the biographies of the Saints we are far more likely to

31

discover for ourselves certain characteristics which lack explanation; there is some deep root influence which we find it beyond our perception to bring to light. Perhaps, it is the fact of our own lack of knowledge of the workings of the Holy Spirit, of the main-springs of human sanctification through the abundance of His Gifts!

Here, too, in the lives of the Saints we are apt to take many of their saintly qualities for granted; and, in their lives, it is often enough the human, rather than the divine, which surprises and attracts us. This is very true, for instance, in the life of St. Francis of Assisi. We take the miracle of the Stigmata for granted; but, his compassion for the sick Brother with whom he eats a bowl of porridge at midnight, surprises and intrigues us; yet, it was the same love manifest in different ways.

However human (and how could their actions be otherwise?) the characteristics are which attract us to a particular Saint, there is always a spiritual motive to account for them. This is not a twisting of facts to make the Saint appear more "pious"; it is simply due to the actuality that he has allowed

the Spirit of God to guide and sway his life. His
Gifts are confirmed in the Saint.

How much more true is this of the Mother of
God! Of all the lesser characteristics of the Virgin
Mother (if we may so distinguish between them),
one which seemingly belonged to her very personally was the gift of spiritual poise or balance.

Poise or balance give a beauty all its own to
personality. Psychologically, it shows a perfection
of character which is, on the whole, rare. It gives
a beauty, if it is natural and not acquired by artifice,
which comes from within the mind and will of
man. It shows command, and yet always signifies
deference towards others. It meets the most difficult situations with a calmness which is far removed
from indifference. It rarely shows excess of any
kind in affection, or in anger; and yet speaks of
tremendous conservation in love, and energy of
mind and will.

All these characteristics, and many others, are
clearly defined in the personality of Mary, the
Mother of God, in the very first instance of our
meeting with her in the Gospels—at the Annunciation. This power of balance or spiritual poise comes

from the Gift of Knowledge imparted by the Holy Spirit of Love. She weighs the words of the divine messenger, feels her own utter inadequacy, seeks enlightenment, finds the divine explanation, gives her humble assent. There is no undue haste, no false humility, no shrinking from terrible responsibilities.

Later, the same traits are manifested to her cousin, Elizabeth; in the presence of one to whom a lesser favor, of the same kind, has been granted, there is the same quiet command, the same humble regard: "Because He who is mighty has done great things for me" (Luke, i. 49).

The Gift of Knowledge is the mainspring of this power of valuation between ourselves and God; between our own resources and limitations and the divine power to work within us; between our will and the will of God. "I can do all things in Him who strengthens me," says St. Paul (Philip., iv. 13), for he has knowledge of himself and knowledge of God's omnipotent will.

It is thus only that we can meet the situations brought about by God's Providence, in such a way as to meet His will, and add to our greater sanctity.

The Gift of Knowlege will make known to us the practical sources of our spiritual life; it will make us realize that these powers come from God, not from ourselves. There will be no undue elation at success, no excess of sadness in failure, no shrinking at assenting to the high vocation to which we are called: "I will fear no evils, for Thou art with me" (Ps., xxii. 4).

# VII

# *Wisdom Without Learning*

*Blessed are they that keep my ways. Hear instruction and be wise, and refuse it not. Blessed is the man that heareth me, and that watcheth daily at my gates, and waiteth at the posts of my doors. He that shall find me shall find life, and shall have salvation from the Lord (Prov., viii. 32-36).*

Such a text as this, and many more, are used in the Liturgy by Holy Mother Church to express the wisdom of the Mother of God. Here, as we shall note elsewhere, Wisdom refers to the supernatural gift of the Holy Spirit of Love.

Whether Mary was greatly learned in the profane or ordinary sciences, we do not know. Many who are learned in this sense of knowing about things, show little wisdom in the real sense of the word. They are often stupid about very practical things, and sometimes disorderly in their lives. They have knowledge without purpose, without a goal of achievement.

Wisdom in the sense of the Liturgy, which is so closely affiliated to our concept of the Mother of God, is fundamentally the source and principle of *order* in our lives. It is a Gift of the Holy Ghost by which we co-ordinate the natural and the supernatural within us; by which we harmonize the natural and the supernatural purposes and goals of life's endeavor.

Wisdom is the third of the Gifts of the Holy Spirit directly influencing the intellect of man; that is, man destined to the supernatural grace of God. A man, in the natural sphere of life, is deemed wise who consistently subordinates the instruments of life to the end and purpose he has in mind. The gifts of mind and body with which he is endowed, the external elements of life (whether persons, places or things), all of these are ordered by the wise man to some high end and purpose which he has made his own.

A man, in the supernatural sphere, is deemed wise who subordinates the instruments of life to the end and purpose revealed to him by God, to the end and purpose for which God, his Creator, made him. Disorder came into man's life with original

37

sin. The more immediate aims of man, his natural purposes in life, gradually crowded out the divine goal of man. He became the victim of flesh and blood, of ambitions and affections which were at variance with the fundamental reason for which he came into this world. There was a conflict, an incongruity and disorder in his life.

When Christ restored to us the gift of eternal and supernatural life with God, He did not fail to give the means of fulfilling that new order in grace. And among the many gifts He gave was the Gift of Wisdom, the direct means of restoring order between the natural and the supernatural.

His Gift, given us through His Spirit of Love, helps us to see the two worlds, this earthly kingdom and the Kingdom of God, through the mind and intentions of God. Wisdom, in this sense, is given to all men who remain in the grace of God. This is the explanation for the trait of sanctity in all classes of men and women. However ignorant they may be in secular affairs, they have had an outstanding power to achieve greatness by so ordering their lives as to acquire renown among the saints, that is, among those who sought and found "first the kingdom of God and His justice."

Wisdom, in the purely human sense, is given to few; Wisdom, in the supernatural sense, is given to all who are called in Christ to a life of grace. This Gift of the Holy Spirit is given to all who are willing to be led by the Spirit of God, to those who are the sons of God and co-heirs with Christ.

The Mother of God had this Gift in a more complete way than any other creature of God. This Gift comes to us when we are very imperfectly fitted to receive it; much has to be done to ensure its perfect operation within us. In Mary, conceived without sin, this jewel of the Holy Spirit found a perfect setting. It came as a crown and new glory to a nature undisturbed by sin. It did not in her have to restore order, as it does in us.

We see this Gift working within the Mother of God on those occasions when the ways of God were not entirely made known to her. She "ponders these things in her heart," she seeks to find the ways of God, to reconcile what seems incongruous with what she knows to be the Will of God. Wisdom does not always mean full understanding of a situation; it *does* mean that *in doubt* we take the best means of disposing ourselves to accept the Eternal Will of God.

It is by the use of this Gift of Wisdom that we shall acquire that peace of mind, that balance of character, which was so marked a feature of the Holy Virgin. St. Augustine has put it in a sentence: "Peace is the tranquillity of order." True order alone comes through seeking God, and disposing all our actions according to His will; for this were we created, to this end was grace restored to us through the inpouring of the Holy Spirit of God. For this reason we were given by Him the graces of faith, hope and charity, that these may find their true fruition in this life, and their permanent reward in the next. It is necessary that we follow the sweet influence of the Holy Spirit of God, who will guide our steps in the ways of His Holy Wisdom; for it is this Gift which will perfect and bring to completion all the others.

# VIII

## Counsels of the Heart

*In all thy works let the true word go before thee, and steady counsel before every action (Ecclus., xxxvii. 20).*

We have considered Wisdom as a Gift of the Holy Ghost which disposes us, in a general way, to shape our lives according to the Will of God. It is Wisdom, in this supernatural sense, which leads us to "seek first the Kingdom of God and His justice" (Matt., vi. 33). Wisdom is the inclination, then, to choose God rather than self, the things of God rather than the things of this world; to choose the eternal rather than the temporal.

However, our eyes are not always inclined towards the eternal hills. Most of us, indeed, have to try to attain heaven with our faculties very much engrossed in the things of this world. In fact, the majority of those whom the Holy Spirit has sanctified, and to whom He has given this Gift of Wisdom, have to fulfill their religious vocation in the world of domestic need, business and everyday affairs.

The same Holy Spirit has, therefore, given them an added spiritual faculty whereby they may follow the dictates of Wisdom, in their everyday vocation.

We referred to Wisdom as the fount or principle of order in our lives. Now, it is the Gift of Counsel which puts the events of our lives exactly "in order."

This is not done by any particular weighing and reasoning about means and end. It is a sharpening of our religious faculty, here and now, to choose this rather than that; to do this thing rather than that; to do some particular action for God rather than leave it undone.

The Gift of Counsel carries Wisdom into the line of action concerning some deed. Wisdom is the light, the eternal light shed on our lives; Counsel is the spot-light which helps to make this particular action, or sacrifice, worth while for the Kingdom of God and His justice.

We hear of men who have a particular faculty, or instinct, for choosing the right moment to buy or sell, to their own advantage. In the supernatural sphere, the Gift of Counsel is just such a power which helps us, under the influence of the Holy Spirit, to choose this moment to do or avoid something thereby acquiring merit for ourselves and giving greater honor and glory to God.

The very ordinariness of the earthly life of the Mother of God, and the fact that we have so brief a reference to her in the Gospels, make it difficult always to illustrate a particular point from her life, at least, without repetition.

Her own words, especially those given us in her ecstatic poem of the *Magnificat,* show us how embued she was with the Gift of Wisdom.

The wisdom of the Mother of God, as far as we are aware, was largely concerned with her own sanctification and the fulfillment of her Divine Maternity. It was in this latter office and duty that she comes so close to all of those who have to live in this vale of tears. It was in this sphere of domestic life that she sanctified herself, and fulfilled the Will of God. It must, therefore, be said of her that the title she bears of Mother of Good Counsel, was won in the incidents of life common to us all. The

Gift of Counsel made her fully aware that the most ordinary events of life are those given us to prepare for the Kingdom of God.

The fact that Mary so seldom obtrudes herself upon our attention in the Holy Gospels, shows us that her sanctification was won very much "behind the scenes." Is this not true of ourselves? And, yet, we know from experience that it is in these matters, "behind the scenes," that we need very sound advice, if we are to turn the events of life to the greatest possible advantage. We are aware time and again, when we examine ourselves, that it is in the ordinary things of life that we have let slide opportunities, let them pass us, without turning them to a meritorious advantage.

If we were practical (and this is the essential work of the Gift of Counsel), we would see the events of the day as a host of opportunities from which to merit a reward. Could we not ask ourselves: "How would the Mother of God meet this situation? How would she deal with this particular obstacle which is constantly cropping up? What would be her attitude to this or that particular person, this type of friendship?"

44

It is by trying to catch a reflection in our own soul of what Mary would do in these particular circumstances, that we are actually using the Gift of Counsel without realizing it. The fact that we turn to her for confirmation, or negation, of what we must do here and now, is itself through the action of this Gift of Counsel influenced by the Holy Spirit of God.

It is thus, to paraphrase a former quotation, that we "watch daily at her gates, and wait at the posts of her doors . . . it is thus that we shall find her, and shall find life, and have salvation from the Lord."

# IX

# *Fear Without Reproach*

*He that feareth the Lord shall tremble at nothing, and shall not be afraid: for He is his hope (Ecclus., xxxiv. 16).*

Fear came into the world with sin. This does not mean that merely to feel fear is a sin. It does mean that as a result of sin, and especially owing to the wound of original sin, we have lost command over things in the world around us, and over some of the powers within us. It is this loss of command that makes us fear physical evil, pain and suffering. Within us there are passions and forces over which we have not full control, and we fear that they may be too strong for us to govern them.

There is nothing which so shrinks the heart of man, which so incapacitates his faculties of mind and body, as fear. Psychologists tell us that most of the complexes and deformities of the mind are related to unknown, but prevalent, fears in the subconscious.

Most of us have seen quiet, strong and beautiful characters changed and distorted by fear; we have seen great purposes and ambitions frustrated and nullified by this emotion; crime is often the result of it; procrastination is its constant companion; meanness and hypocrisy manifest its presence. Fear is the cause of barrenness of effort; it stultifies the mind and impedes any noble aspirations; before it, the will becomes enfeebled, and all adventure is considered a labyrinth of uncertitudes and potential failures.

Fear, then, is the enemy and opposite of virtue. Where fear is ruling, we do not look for goodness, for any form of generosity of purpose; nor is there room for charity; there is no peace, no kind of security.

The greatest calumny against religion is that it has its origin in fear. This is an oft-repeated profanation of truth, however cleverly it may be illustrated by supposed rites and ceremonies of primitive peoples. Religion has nothing in common with fear, as we have tried to define and illustrate it above; nor with that emotion or repulsion of the will which we may find more readily within ourselves. Religion means a re-binding *with* our Creator; fear is a fleeing *from* Him. St. John witnesses to two religious truths: "God is Love," and "Love casts out fear," he declares (I John, iv. 16, 18).

Yet, we must admit that the word "fear" has a very prominent place in religious writings and the revealed word of God. It is very frequently used in regard to man's relationship with God: "Fear the Lord . . . Fear . . . is the beginning of wisdom" (Deut., vi. 24; Ps. cx. 10). Among the Seven Gifts of the Holy Spirit of Love is the Gift of the Fear of the Lord. How then reconcile this seeming contradiction: "fear" the source of most that is ignoble in man, and "fear" the beginning of wisdom, the basis of all true and solid virtue?

Human fear is an emotion, the offspring of hate: divine, holy fear is the fruit of love. Here, love, is the clue to the answer to our question.

The Gift of Holy Fear presupposes the basis of supernatural union with God—grace, divine charity. It is a movement, a quality or divine influence that causes us to cling to God as our All. It is, as regards the *mind*, an "appreciation" of His infinite goodness and power, so that we would suffer (it is, therefore, a strong, self-sacrificing virtue) anything rather than be separated from Him. It is, as regards the *will*, a tenderness lest we be attached to anything contrary to God's will; a tenderness lest anything draw us away from the Source of all our goodness, and the Object of our love.

Holy Fear is obviously founded in humility, in a true recognition of our lowliness and of God's greatness. In this it is the beginning of all wisdom; the beginning of wisdom is the appreciation of our own ignorance, of God's infinitude of wisdom.

Holy Fear is clearly the source of all security and peace of mind, for it makes us cling, by faith, to the all-sufficiency of God, our Father. It is the mainspring of generosity and fraternal charity, for it is born in love. It is the beginning of all-holy ambition, purposefulness, for it holds fast to the hand of God; it has no fear of evil without, it can go forward undeterred, for it feels and rests in the strength of God.

Mirrored in the soul of Mary the Virgin we find much to admire and imitate. Nothing would seem to be more incongruous than to discover a shadow of that *human* fear, which we first considered. We

49

shall, however, see there a clear reflection of that Holy Fear of the Lord, given her through the Gift of Divine Love.

"How shall this be done?" (Luke, i. 34). This is a question prompted by Holy Fear. It does not arise out of any human fear of responsibility of motherhood, out of any shrinking from the self-sacrifice that such a vocation entails. It is moved by the Holy Fear of an apparent conflict between two loves: one of God, to whom Mary is united by a vow of virginity, and that love which would be given to her Son. Holy Fear prompts the question; Wisdom finds the answer. Holy Fear, the handmaid of humility, causes Mary to be disturbed at the title given her by the Angel Gabriel, who answers her thought by the words: "Do not be afraid, Mary, for thou hast found grace with God" (Luke, i. 30).

The courage of Mary, in the sense that the human emotion of fear was conquered, is clearly indicated by her manner of facing the anxieties of the journey to and hardship of Bethlehem. The same courage is manifest in the difficulties and the fortitude with which she faced the exile in Egypt, when she had to shield her Son from His first human persecutor. Ordinary human fear finds no place in this Mother's heart, as she stands beside her Son in the midst of that crowd on Calvary.

Here, indeed, it was holy fear of God which made her cling, by faith, to the all-sufficiency of God, our Father; here was a darkness of mind which could only be pierced by faith. Holy Fear of God's unsearchable ways alone could hold back the cry of this Mother, for the awful thing that sin had done to her Son.

In Mary, Holy Fear and love of God are entirely one: in us, though Holy Fear is born of love, the grace of God, there is not always this close union. Though born of love, this Gift of the Spirit of Love has often to play the part of guardian to our union with God. It helps us appreciate in our darkest hours the infinite power and goodness of God; it prepares us to suffer anything rather than separation from Him. It is the beginning of wisdom, the handmaid of charity, the pledge of final perseverance.

## X

# Orphans No Longer

*I will be to him a father, and he shall be to me a son (Heb., i. 5).*

Though the concept and acknowledgment of the Fatherhood of God is made known in the Old Testament and Jewish tradition, it is true that this aspect of the Godhead did not manifest itself to the same extent as did others in the rites and writings of the Chosen People.

Only when the Son of God came on earth with the fullness of the Revelation, do we receive an adequate knowledge of God's Fatherhood. In the New Testament, the New Covenant between God and His people, we come to appreciate the fullness of the meaning of "Our Father who art in heaven." Directly, and indirectly, Christ reveals to us the new relationship between man and his Maker. It is through His merits and the sanctification of the Spirit of Love that we become the adopted sons of

God, and co-heirs with Christ, the Only Begotten of the Father.

Time and again Christ demonstrates the reality of this new relationship with the Eternal Father. Not only is this true in the words and parables He uses to bring this truth home to us; but the means of sanctification which He commands us to use, focus our attention upon our condition as children of God, and His Fatherhood of us.

We are to be born again of water and the Holy Spirit that we may become truly the children of God. This rebirth by the renewed power of God, is absolutely necessary for salvation. We are commanded under the most solemn dictate of Christ to eat of His Flesh and to drink of His Blood, so that we may have life with our Father: "Amen, Amen, I say to you; Moses did not give you the true bread from heaven . . . As the living Father has sent me, and as I live because of the Father, so he who eats me, he also shall live because of me" (and through me live by the Father). The Advent of the Holy Spirit was to confirm this union with the Father and the Son: "You have received a spirit of adoption as sons, by virtue of which we cry 'Abba! Father!' The Spirit himself gives testimony to our spirit, that we are the sons of God" (Rom., viii. 15 sq.).

St. Paul, the great apostle of charity, in the eighth chapter of Romans, continues to stress the filial love which is given to us by the Holy Spirit, that we may more fully appreciate our place as the adopted sons of God; that this doctrine may become a greater and greater reality to us.

It is as if God feared that this idea would be too novel to us; as if we would always feel that we were His children on sufferance, rather than by that union of grace which is the closest relationship we can ever have towards God. St. Peter expresses this truth in startling terms calling the union of grace, a participation in the divine nature (II Pet., i. 4).

To insure that we may feel perfectly "at home" as the adopted sons of God, the Holy Spirit has, by Confirmation, embedded within us a special spiritual influence, an instinct by which we may at all times realize and feel that we are truly the children of God, and He is our Father. This is the Gift of Piety, of Filial Love.

No one of the Seven Gifts of the Holy Ghost

has received less attention than this one. This, more than any other Gift, has been most unfortunately affected by the mischance of the corruption of words.

The word "piety" has come to mean anything, rather than the simple love of a son for his father. It has become confused with a certain, and unfortunate, religiosity associated with women who observe only the externals of religion.

The Gift of Piety is not the same as the virtue of religion. This latter is a debt of justice to God, as the Over-Lord of all things. Piety goes far beyond the call of justice; it has a great content of charity. It does not stop at the fulfillment of Commandments, it reaches out to the Counsels of perfection. It searches out the ways and means of closer union with the Son of God, that we may be recognized by the Father as His sons in Christ, and share eternal life with Him, and be one with the love of the Holy Spirit.

Piety makes us easily responsive to the inspirations of the Spirit of Love; makes us agile in the fulfillment of the will of our Father, while we are on earth, as His will is fulfilled in heaven. It is a

robust and reverent regard towards God, recognizing all that the Father has done to rescue us from
evil, to claim us as His own, to deliver "us from the
power of darkness, and transfer us into the kingdom of his beloved Son" (Col., i. 13).

If this spiritual instinct of filial love is now strong
within us, so that we take it almost for granted,
how strong and enduring must it not have been in
her who bears the title, Mother of God! The unique
relationship between the Virgin of Nazareth and
the Word of God manifests how close must have
been her union with the Eternal Father, after the
overshadowing of the Holy Spirit of God.

But, it is quite evident that, if we prescind from
the stupendous privilege which Mary had through
the consummation of the Mystery of the Incarnation, she gave every evidence of that spiritual characteristic of filial piety on a plane more in common
with our own.

The poem of the *Magnificat,* to which we have
already referred more than once, breathes much of
this regard and reverence for God, our Father. The
whole of her attitude during the episode of the
Annunciation is of one waiting upon the will of

God: "Behold the handmaid of the Lord, be it done to me according to thy word." There is no false humility of unworthiness, no undue timidity to accept such a tremendous office from God. There is true humility joined with eagerness to fulfill what is required of her. There is holy fear, yet a strong resolution to do and follow the will of God in all things.

From no one could we better ask for, and no one could we better strive to imitate in this filial devotion, which springs from the Gift of Piety, given us by the Paraclete. It is required of us in a unique manner, because by grace we bear the image of the Son of God, which gives us a title to call His Father, our Father who art in heaven.

# XI

# Meeting A Challenge

*Restore unto me the joy of thy salvation, and strengthen me with a perfect spirit (Ps., l. 14).*

The sign of the Christian is the sign of the Cross. It is not only a sign of suffering, though the imagination readily flies to the image of a suffering Figure when considering this symbol of our holy religion. It is, also, a sign of guilt. Much more is it a sign of conquest.

However we may be helped by the other Gifts of the Holy Spirit to see and to understand the high vocation and the intimate relationship we have as children of God, little will be done in its fulfillment and perfection unless knowledge is supplemented by resolution.

The Cross is a challenge. The Gifts of Knowledge, Understanding, Counsel and Wisdom play their appointed place in the appreciation of what the Cross means to us; whether as regards our own part in its sign of guilt, whether in the recognition of our own due share to be taken in reparation through penance and suffering, or in the hope of our conquest through the merits of Christ. These concern an attitude of mind. These Gifts enable us to penetrate the mystery of the Cross, which to the pagan mind is a sign of shame or of folly. The Cross is a challenge to modern and ancient thought, which is so concerned with the ways and means of present and earthly happiness. The Gifts of the Holy Spirit enable us to meet and solve that problem of pain, that challenge of the Cross to our eternal good.

But the Cross is, even more, a challenge to the will of man. The Gifts, with which we have been concerned, may well show us the true Christian attitude towards guilt, suffering and sacrifice, but the will may shrink from the effort which will be required to make the Christian attitude something more than an ideal to be attained.

The Holy Spirit, who is perfect in all His works, has not left this weakness unaided in His attention to our needs. The Gift of Fortitude is there within us to be the bulwark which will protect us against ourselves. Both the weakness and the remedy lie within us. The courage of Fortitude comes from a thorough knowledge of ourselves; it is accompanied with a like knowledge of the source of spiritual strength: God Himself.

Wisdom will teach us to solve the weakness of nature and the strength of the supernatural. Understanding will penetrate the innate power of the weapons which God has placed in our hands, the power coming from God alone. Both of these considerations will bolster the will to face and overcome the difficulties, and the sacrifices involved in the issue. But the Holy Spirit does not leave it to this indirect and supernatural influence of the mind upon the will to accomplish the task of restoration which He has given us to perform. The Gift of Fortitude is a more direct influence on the will than any other weapon we possess in our spiritual armor. It inclines the will to a direct acceptation of the Cross in the warfare of the soul against the devil, the world and the flesh. It is an influence which ensures perseverance; it helps the individual to meet the tussles between nature and the supernatural in such a way that conquest in this struggle is made with greater ease and skill. As the mind, under the influence of the Gifts of the Spirit, presents new fields of spiritual conquest, the Gift of Fortitude stimulates the will to accept rather than shrink from the effort involved.

The Gift of Fortitude is distinguished from the virtue in so far as the former is present for immediate action or necessity, rather than being a store of reserved spiritual power. The Gift of Fortitude is given us to meet the challenge of Christ, that we take up our cross *daily* and follow Him. It is a support and reinforcement for daily action, just as Counsel is for our practical knowledge to do or not to do. How great a part, then, must it play in the working out of our way of perfection!

It might well seem that the Gift of Fortitude would be unnecessary in the development of the spiritual life of the Mother of God. In the first place, there was in her no original wound from the injury of original sin. There was, therefore, no need for a work of coöperation in the sense of restoration. Then, her union with God by grace, and she was "full of grace," was so close that we would find it hard, and be pushing an analogy too far, to

61

call her conformity with God's grace a "struggle." Concupiscence, evil tendencies, unrestrained passions were unknown to her who was "conceived without sin." There would seem to be little room, therefore, for the need of fortitude as we have considered it.

Fortitude is not merely a Gift to remedy past evil, or succor present weakness; it enables us to persevere in merit. Even though Mary was full of grace, there was still the possibility for her to merit. Merit comes through trial, either in a duty fulfilled, or a difficulty to be overcome.

It was in this sense that Mary responded to the Gift of the Holy Spirit, the Gift of Fortitude. The trials and difficulties of her life were many; we have already mentioned not a few. The mental anguish of the separation from her Son for three days; His bewildering answer to her question on that occasion; the sufferings she endured at His being rebuffed by His own people, even His own townfolk; the terrible trial of the Passion and Death; the long wait between His Ascension and her own Assumption into heaven. All of these trials called for fortitude of the highest order, even in one who had been perfected by grace, and who was untainted by the weakness of sin.

Perseverance can only become fruitful in the unknown future; our present state is connected with that future state of final tranquillity by a long series of acts of the will, which should be acts of love. The guardian and support of each of those acts, multiplied a million times in a life-time, is the Gift of Fortitude, given by that Spirit who confirmed us one day, many years ago. May He confirm us unto the day of salvation!

# XII

## *Mystery Incarnate*

*It is she that teacheth the knowledge of God, and is the chooser of his works (Wis., viii. 4).*

So far we have considered the mysterious workings of the Holy Spirit in the soul; we have reflected upon the operation of the Holy Ghost in the Immaculate Heart of Mary, whom He chose as His Spouse.

We know from the revealed word of God, and from the sacred tradition of the Church, that the Holy Spirit of God had other purposes in His holy operation beyond the personal sanctification of Mary's soul. We know that, from the moment the Maid of Nazareth consented to be the Spouse of the Holy Ghost, she would be forever bound up in the Mystery of the Incarnation. It was inevitable that she should be associated in our minds and hearts with the Mysteries of the Divine Infancy, with the chief events of the Incarnate Word of

God on earth. From the moment that Christ bequeathed His Mother to the care of the Beloved Disciple, it was certain that we would think of her in connection with the infant days of His Church. Further, the sacred tradition of the Church, its history and unfolding power, have made known to us the intimate and familiar place that Mary has had in the Mysteries of the Mystical Body of Christ, her Divine Son. We know that this latter work of God may be attributed directly to the manifold power of the Holy Spirit, who was to be sent into the world to consummate the mission and revelation of the Son of God on earth.

We would have an insufficient picture in our mind of the workings of the Holy Spirit in regard to the Mother of Jesus, if we restricted our attention to His inward sanctification of her soul. Mary was to enter into the Mysteries of the Incarnate Word made known to us on earth, and also into the Mysteries of the Mystical Body of Christ through the Divine Spirit of Wisdom. Her Divine Motherhood was to embrace far more than the physical aspects of the Incarnation. Or rather, through being the Spouse of the Holy Ghost, Her Motherhood concerned all that is wonderful in God being with us. Through sanctification He is with us to this day; through the Gifts of the Holy Spirit, through faith, hope and charity, we know, love and serve Him; through His Mysteries He dwells with us; and through the inpouring of the Holy Spirit, the Word is born within us, even as we are reborn unto salvation and the Kingdom of God.

History and sacred tradition have made known to us the intimate part that Mary has played in these recurring Mysteries of God among men. The evidence of ages is so overwhelming that we cannot miss the significance of Mary's position and office in the building up of the Mystical Body of Her Son, even as she was God's handmaid in giving herself in the formation of His physical body. She has witnesses in every age, and in every class of society, to the power she has as advocate; to the inspiration she has been to those who are striving to put on Jesus Christ, to bear the image of her Son in their souls. The Liturgy of the Church is resplendent with feasts in her honor, each witnessing to some new intervention of hers on behalf of man.

The Paraclete, the Spirit of Truth, has made

known to us age by age that His Spouse, and the Mother of the Word, has been given a special place in the winning of souls to redemption. It could have been otherwise; God could have dispensed with any further services of His handmaid; but it is His will to make her name loved and honored from generation to generation, and that all men should call her blessed.

Deep-rooted in the traditions of Catholic action in every age, in the unfolding of the Mercies of God, is the figure of Mary. It is only for us to discover the place and presence of this Holy Virgin for ourselves; to give praise to God that the Holy Spirit still regards the "necessity" of using the Virgin of Nazareth to make known to men in our day the splendors of His graces, the holiness of those who are called to be, and are, the sons of God. .

# XIII

# *The First Joy*

*Be glad with her, all you that love her; rejoice for joy with her (Isa., lxvi. 10).*

There is a constitutional ring about the word happiness. It is an echo of the document which gives the foundation to the American way of life; the phrase used is "the pursuit of happiness." Philosophers and theologians are agreed, for the most part, that this pursuit is an innate striving of man, something born within him, a movement of his being from which he cannot escape.

They who seek and, in part, find this happiness possess a special mark of joyousness. It is a conscious possession of the threads of happiness, quite distinct from any sense of smugness. It may be manifest in those who, seemingly, have little else to boast of by way of possessions. It is more often reflected in the eyes of the poor than in those of the rich; it often appears after great sacrifices have been made in a

68

bid for happiness; it is the joy of those who have been in labor, and have found rest. We have said that one of the lost virtues of the world of to-day is the virtue of hope. With the loss of hope one other gift in life has been lost, the gift of joy.

If our literature and our songs are any indication and reflection of human ideal (and who shall doubt this?), then "joy" is as dead as the dodo. And "joy" is the note of happiness possessed. Something else has been substituted for happiness; it is called pleasure. They write and sing of "the pleasure of being in your arms"; that is where pleasure belongs, to the senses, to the stimulation of passion. Joy belongs to the soul; it can shine through tears; we can be joyful without *feeling* any pleasure. Joy is content of the spirit. We speak of the spirit of joy, and we are right; far more accurate than the writer is about pleasure being a substitute for happiness. Joy is a possession of the spirit of man, and no false pleasure (that is false happiness) can rob him of it. True joy was expressed in the poem of the Maid of Nazareth: "My soul doth magnify the Lord; and my spirit hath rejoiced in God my Savior." It is

Mary, the Cause of our Joy, who can teach us most about this gift of God.

"Rejoice, thou barren that dost not bear; break forth and cry, thou that dost not travail; for many are the children of the desolate, more than of her that has a husband" (Gal., iv. 27). St. Paul uses these words of the prophet Isaias directly to show the nature of our rebirth in Christ. They may, however, be used concerning the Mother of God.

Isaias was inspired in many of his words by the Holy Spirit of God concerning the mystery of the Word made Flesh. His words throw much light upon the secrets of the overshadowing of the Holy Spirit at the Annunciation. Isaias is, in these words, directly referring to the nations of the Gentiles, who, through no possible power or experience of their own, could come to a knowledge of God Incarnate, yet would, through His will, bring forth innumerable sons of God. And how aptly these same words may be applied to the Virgin of Nazareth!

By the inspiration of God, and her own choice, she is vowed to virginity. She will never bear children according to the "will of man"; she will, in fact, never know travail. Then God, through the overshadowing of the Holy Spirit, decrees that she shall be the Mother of His Only Begotten Son; and, through this Son, shall be the Mother of all of those who are reborn in the likeness of Christ by grace. In this sense the Virgin is a thousand times more fruitful than any human mother.

Here, indeed, are manifest the mysterious ways of God; Mary denies herself the greatest joy and expectation of a Jewish maiden: to be a mother, and perhaps, God willing, the chosen one to bear the Messiah, the Promised Savior. Mary denies herself all human possibility of this joy by her vow of virginity. God, in His inscrutable wisdom, chooses this same Virgin to be the Mother of His Son. God will not deny her the joy she denies herself; rather, will He multiply her joys a thousandfold.

Spiritual joy, as we have suggested, is the conscious possession of happiness, which is best expressed in love. It is so closely allied to charity that we can only speak of it as an effect of love possessed. It is a direct fruit of the Spirit of Love, a fruit of the virtue of charity and the Gift of Piety. And because spiritual joy, as opposed to merely natural human pleasure, is a part of love, it can embrace suffering. In this most certainly joy is different from "pleasure," which can be expressed in suffering only if it is perverted. Joy, bound together with love, can surmount suffering and accept it, recognizing it as a purification, an immolation of self, on the altar of love. Joy is made of sterner and more constant stuff than pleasure, which is allied to feeling and the inconstancies of the flesh. Yes, joy is a thing of the spirit; it can be, and is meant to be, one of the immortal fruits of the Spirit of Love.

We find this spiritual joy manifest in the often-quoted *Magnificat*. We can detect its presence on many other occasions in the Gospel life of Mary. It is something which she imparted to others; for, like her love, it was expansive and expressive. "For behold, the moment that the sound of thy greeting came to my ears, the babe in my womb leapt for joy" (Luke, i. 44). The joy of Mary's Motherhood was vibrant in her voice; it stirred the unborn life of another. The message of the Annunciation, even before it was consummated in the Birth of the Savior, was one of joy, as the angel was to declare that it would be: "Do not be afraid, for behold, I bring you good news of great joy which shall be to all the people" (Luke, ii. 10).

This mystery of the overshadowing of the Holy Spirit at the Annunciation has brought to life a new-found joy in the sterile womb of nature. The voice of Mary has reawakened in barren ages, and barren hearts, the joy of the Savior's Coming. The mother love and joy of this Maiden have brought forth a new note of expectancy. Her love and her joy have brought, into the hearts of those disillusioned by pleasure, a new regard for a love deeper, more constant and joyous. A love born of the Spirit has come into the lives of those whom the Mother of God has influenced: a recreation by the Spirit of God of mind and heart, so that they may bear within them the Image of the Son of God, and bring forth fruit in patience; one of the fruits being spiritual joy in the Lord.

## XIV

# A Vacation in the Hills

*While the King was at his repose, my spikenard sent forth the odor thereof (Cant., i. 11).*

It is with all due reverence that we speak of the Mystery of the Visitation as a vacation. It was, in fact, just that. As an episode in the unfolding of the Mystery of the Incarnation, it is an "aside" in the great drama of the Birth of our Savior. Looking at it with the simple eyes of faith and an unaffected piety, it was a holiday for the Mother of God in the hills of Judea. St. Luke with deep understanding of feminine nature, and as an exact narrator of revealed truth, tells us of this journey and the joyous giving of congratulation to her cousin Elizabeth. The visit falls in the months between the tremendous revelation of the Annunciation and the Manifestation of the Savior in Bethlehem. In one sense, it has so little to do with the great wonders of the Divine Mystery of God

coming to men that we might well have expected
the Evangelist to hurry on to the immediate history
of Christ's birth. Indeed, that is what the other
holy writers did do. But how much poorer in
knowledge we, of another generation, would have
been if St. Luke had not written this story for us!
He is the most explicit writer concerning Mary, the
Spouse of the Holy Ghost. This "aside" of his is full
of Mary and the Holy Spirit.

We are not told that Mary was directly inspired
by the Holy Ghost to visit her cousin at this time,
nor would we expect her to make his long and difficult journey during her expectancy. Elizabeth is
full of joyful surprise at her coming: "How have
I deserved that the mother of my Lord should come
to me?" (Luke, i. 43). Though there is no reason to
assume that the Virgin was directly guided by the
Holy Spirit, nevertheless it was by the quiet impulse of the Holy Ghost that she did so.

What is it that impels Mary to fulfill this act of
charity towards her aged and less favored cousin?
We would say in our natural idiom that she did so
out of the goodness of her heart. In those words are
contained a volume of meaning. How often we use

this expression of one whom we hold in affection, of one who is constant in small acts of charity, which add up to so much in life! So common is the phrase we do not realize that we are uncovering one of the mysterious workings of the Spirit of Love in the human soul. But so it is. "Goodness of heart" is one of the fruits of the Spirit. It is more common than we imagine; and so is the influence of the Holy Spirit. Where we see goodness, whether it is at the hands of some good Sister in a hospital or it is seen shining in the grimed faces of the neighborly poor, we are looking upon the fruit of the Spirit of Love. It is an inspiration to think that He is so near us, though we do not always recognize Him in the disguise He assumes.

Out of the goodness of her heart, thus indirectly moved by the Spirit of God, Mary pays the visit to her cousin. In this friendly, almost prosaic episode, a greater manifestation of the Spirit is made known to us. Two mothers meet at a cottage door, the one young, the other advanced in years. They share in the secret of their maternity, the hidden wonders of God; for one is a virgin, the other long past the due course of maternity. Both women have been visited by the creative power of God, and are filled with His Holy Spirit. "And Elizabeth was filled with the Holy Spirit; and cried with a loud voice saying, 'Blessed art thou among women, and blessed is the fruit of thy womb'" (Luke, i. 42). This cry has been echoed by the generations of men, women and children, who have added the name, "Jesus."

The Holy Spirit of God has given us in His own words of inspiration the comparison of these two mothers, by which we might ponder upon the wonder of His works. The Holy Ghost makes use of these two historic and exceptional motherhoods to show how close He is to the work of His hands. To use the words of one who has recorded this scene, "we ask ourselves whether it is possible for a woman to have God nearer to her in joys of maternity, than it is conveyed by that wonderful proximity of heaven in the origin of John's life." We know from the Visitation that it *was* possible to have an even closer union, even in the physical fact, for Mary bore within her the very Living God Himself.

Again, the Holy Spirit of God makes this passing and unexpected visit of Mary, this vacation, a reward of faith. How unexpected He is in His wondrous rewards! Mary had asked, on the occasion of the Annunciation, for no external sign to confirm the message of the angel. She had sought only the solution of conscience: how in conscience this thing might be, that a virgin might bear a son. Yet, a sign was given her: "And behold, Elizabeth thy kinswoman also has conceived a son in her old age, and she who was called barren is now in her sixth month; for nothing shall be impossible with God" (Luke, i. 36). Mary accepts this sign, even without waiting confirmation of the news. When these mothers meet, when Mary witnesses the sign by which she would know that she was indeed the Spouse of the Holy Ghost, Elizabeth, inspired by the same Spirit, bears witness to her cousin's faith: "Blessed art thou that hast believed, because those things shall be accomplished that were spoken to thee by the Lord" (Luke, i. 45).

Thus, goodness of heart and faith, the fruit of charity and the light of virtue, seeds of the Spirit of Love, find their unexpected rewards in the Visitation of Mary, a vacation in the hills of Judea, over which was to ring so soon a new hymn to welcome the Child she bore during this interlude of joy in the Holy Ghost: "Glory to God in the highest, and peace on earth among men of good will" (Luke, ii. 14).

# XV

# Bethlehem

*When the fullness of time was come (Gal., iv. 4).*

Once a year all over the world the bells of Christmas announce the anniversary of the Savior's Birth. Men, women and children make special preparation both in soul and body to celebrate becomingly the Feast Day of the Christ-Child. Those who thus prepare themselves can be counted in their tens of millions; they are of every race of mankind, of every class and color, of every age and condition of life.

Considering the immense space of time, the long history of centuries that went before this supreme event, it is astounding that in so short a time, and to such a universal extent, there should be this global recognition of the Savior's Birthday. Only the most illuminated faith, only a supernatural knowledge, could have foreseen and foretold that the Son born of Mary of Nazareth in Bethlehem of Judea on that December night would receive these Birth-day tributes nineteen hundred years later in lands and by peoples then unknown and undiscovered.

To the Mother, who so joyfully gave birth to this Son, this future of His was in part revealed by the messenger of God: "He shall be great, and shall be called the Son of the Most High; and the Lord God will give him the throne of David his father, and he shall be king over the house of Jacob forever; and of his kingdom there shall be no end" (Luke, i. 32). His Maiden-Mother must have recalled, if they were not ever present to her mind, these words when the shepherds brought their story of the vision of angels over Bethlehem: "But Mary kept in mind all these words, pondering them in her heart" (Luke, ii. 19).

We must not forget that Mary also knew that this Child, whom she named Jesus (Savior), stood as one alone against the world. Though the Jewish people might read prophecy aright, and accept him to the throne of David their father, what of the world without?

May we not ask the same question to-day? To the abounding world of men and women of the world to-day Christmas is a *Christian* Feast. It is a celebration which belongs to a select body of believers; it belongs to a specific body of men and women who have and feel special alliances, special loyalties, to the Christ-Child. While, from a social and civic aspect, others experience the effects of the Holyday, while even some of the religious joy and fervor of Christians may touch their lives, they do not feel that this is *their* day of celebration. To them, if they think of this aspect at all, it is the Natal Day of the Christian Savior, of *a* Savior, not *the* Savior; much less *their* Savior. They do not feel that they owe their salvation specifically to Him; they do not feel that they have been saved. In this sense, they feel about Christmas much the same as non-American residents feel about Independence Day or Thanksgiving Day. However much they may join in the social and civic celebrations, its freedom from labor and jollity, they do not enter into the heart of the day, they do not feel the historic affinities and the loyalties as do the citizens; it does not touch *their* patriotism. They cannot enter into the heart of America's Natal Day, because it is not *their* freedom which was won long ago. In a word, such strangers cannot enter into the *spirit* of such a national holiday.

When we speak of the "spirit" of Christmas, we may mean one of a hundred things, even things contrary one to another. What we should mean is what makes Christmas truly a universal Natal Day. This is the fact that Christ was not *a* Savior, but *the* Savior of mankind. In this sense, it is not a mere sectarian Holyday; in this sense, it is not merely a Christian Feast.

Men will not make Christmas entirely theirs, will not feel its true joy, its loves, its freedom, above all, its peace, until they have made the Christ-Child their Savior. And it is a truism to say that they will not do this until they feel the need and effects of salvation.

Though Mary presents the Savior of the world to mankind in the Mystery of the Nativity, something more is needed that He may be accepted by all men; men must feel the first need of personal salvation and sanctification, and feeling this need, seek that it be satisfied.

When the Christ-Child grew into the fullness of manhood, and showed forth His Divine Person, He spoke very clearly of this need. He spoke about a need and a change which would enable men to enter into the reality of the mystery of salvation. And, strangely enough, He spoke of this change in the terms and words of a nativity, a new birth.

"Amen, amen, I say to thee, unless a man be born again, he cannot see the kingdom of God . . . Unless a man be born again of water and the Spirit, he cannot enter into the kingdom of God . . . Do not wonder that I say to thee, 'You must be born again.' The wind blows where it will, and thou hearest its sound but dost not know where it comes from or where it goes. So is everyone who is born of the Spirit" (John, iii. 3-7).

The fullness of the Mystery of the Savior's Birth, then, is incomplete without the mystery of man's rebirth by the Holy Spirit. It is the love of the Father who gives us His Son; it is the Spirit of Love, breathing where He will, who completes the Mystery.

The Nativity of Christ can mean so much, or so little, according to the presence of the Holy Spirit, who was sent to teach us all truth. To be reborn in the Spirit is to realize our close association with the Birth of the Savior; only in so far as the Spirit of Love is born in the hearts of men, can they feel and know the loyalties, the joys and peace to be given to us by the Christ-Child. The spirit of Christmas is the Spirit of Love; without it we are as strangers celebrating the Birthday of One without that intimacy which comes from being a member of the family.

# XVI

# Light and Shadow

*That the thoughts of many hearts may be revealed (Luke, ii. 35).*

In the midst of the Mysteries of Mary's Joys there appears, for the first time, the shadow of the Cross.

We can only follow the unfolding of the Mystery of the Incarnation which surrounds the Mother of God, in so far as the Holy Spirit chooses to make it known to us. Nor must we be surprised, for it was in this manner, step by step, that Mary came fully to realize the nature of God's plan for her Son, in which she was to take such a personal share.

Incidents in the Divine Infancy seem to catch the Virgin of Nazareth unawares, though they do not by this fact disturb the balance and the simple reliance of her will upon the Will of God. But these sudden shafts of light make known to her the greater depths of God's designs; sometimes they give her only fleeting sight of the sorrow, pain and tragedy to come, and this puzzles and momentarily disturbs her peace and joy. Each greater and more definite revelation comes to her directly or indirectly through the Spirit of God, whose Spouse she is.

The Holy Temple of God is made the scene and setting for one such revealing instance of Mary's greater awakening to the fuller drama of the life of her Son. We, who have God dwelling on our altars day by day, are apt to miss the significance of the Presentation in the Temple. It is not as if Mary took her Son to the synagogue, as it were to the parish church, to present Him to the priest, and to be purified after childbirth. It was much more like taking Him to St. Peter's in Rome! The Temple in Jerusalem was not just a well-known place of worship; it was the very center, and only center, of Jewish sacrificial worship. The Temple was a holy place to which thousands flocked every year; they came from the four corners of the known world. In this place alone was sacrifice offered at sunrise and sunset for the whole people; it was here that the chief priests, the pontiffs, lived and administered to the Jews throughout the world. Going to

87

the Temple was, indeed, a great and solemn occasion.

There, in the sacred precincts of the Temple, Mary offers her Divine Son to the Eternal Father, offering at the same time the gift of sacrifice usual among the poor—a pair of turtle-doves or two young pigeons—as a sign of buying Him back.

It would seem that, when these rites of the Old Law had been fulfilled, the Holy Spirit of God thereupon chose to make a special manifestation of His will concerning the new-born Child. We are told by St. Luke, (ii. 25 sq.) that at this juncture a venerable old man, named Simeon, now, led by the Spirit, came into the temple . . . and, taking the Child from His mother, held Him in his own arms and blessed God in these memorable words: "Now thou dost dismiss thy servant, O Lord, according to thy word, in peace [by the Spirit it had been revealed to him that he was not to meet death, until he had seen that Christ whom the Lord had anointed]; Because my eyes have seen thy salvation, which thou hast prepared before the face of all peoples: A light of revelation to the Gentiles, and a glory for thy people Israel." Seeing how embarrassed the parents were and the puzzled look upon the face of Mary and Joseph, Simeon turns to the mother, and explains his words of praise to God.

The holy man now passes from praise to prophecy, and thus the Holy Spirit uses him to convey a new message to Christ's Immaculate Mother: "Behold, this child is destined to bring about the fall and rise of many in Israel; to be a sign which men will refuse to acknowledge; and so the thought of many hearts shall be made manifest; as for thy own soul, it shall have a sword to pierce it" (Luke, ii. 34).

We can, in no way, gauge the joy which must have filled Mary's heart because this Child, whom she has so lately given to the world, should have been thus publicly singled out by this venerable and esteemed old man. Up to this moment recognition of her Divine Son had only been made by the angels and shepherds; now, it was one of the most highly esteemed of her own people who recognizes Him as "The Light of the world." First Gabriel, then Elizabeth, now Simeon, each through the Holy Spirit adds something new to the manifestation of the divine character of the Child to whom she has given birth. The Holy Ghost, at each new revelation, confirms and strengthens her initial and simple faith. He does so, not only as a reward, but also because He is preparing her for a more difficult rôle in the drama of our salvation.

Following this recognition of the Child's character of Savior, Simeon adds a new light of revelation upon His future, a light which casts a shadow: "This child is destined for the fall and the rise of many in Israel, and for a sign that shall be contradicted. And thy own soul a sword shall pierce" (Luke, ii. 35).

This is the first sign of the Cross. How gently the Holy Spirit of God suggests to Mary, that, though her joy is great because of the future glory of her Son, yet it will not be without the discipline of contradiction and suffering! Here the Holy Spirit gives no more than a hint of what is to come; it is the first of His revelations which will prepare her for the tremendous sorrows that must come to her. Note the veiled language of the message; the Spirit of God does not wish to disturb all peace and joy, but just to hint at—to cause her to think and ponder upon—the price that must be paid for all love worthy of the name.

Mary leaves this unforgettable scene in the holiness of the Temple, full of joy and gratitude, yet pondering ever more deeply upon the hidden ways of God; ever more alert to what the Spirit of Love may demand and ask of her as the price of His love and the dignity of her motherhood.

The Cross does not necessarily cast out joy, for, as we have seen, joy is the fruit of charity; and there is no love of Christ without the Cross which He embraced for love of us.

# XVII

# *The Divine Truant*

*I sought him, and found him not; I called, and he did not answer me (Cant., v. 6).*

We catch only one glimpse of Jesus in His early youth, and the episode in which we hear His voice for the first time is one of peculiar interest and beauty. Many artists have used their talents and imagination to depict for us the scene of Jesus at the age of twelve, sitting in the midst of the Doctors, listening to them and asking them questions. The age of twelve must not deceive us into thinking of Him as a mere child. St. Luke opens his description of this event by summing up the period covered by the years between the Presentation and this going up to the Temple by the Holy Family. He says: ". . . and so the child grew and came to his strength, full of wisdom; and the grace of God rested on him" (Luke ii. 40). Twelve was the age when Jewish boys put aside the things of their

childhood, and prepared to enter into their manhood. The very fact that He was even allowed into
the circle of such learned men, shows how He had
advanced in age, and had the bearing of one above
His years.

While Jesus remained behind in Jerusalem, His
Mother experienced her first great sorrow concerning Him. The flight and exile in Egypt had
been a time of much anxiety. Simeon's prophecy,
that her Child would be a sign of contradiction,
and one which men would refuse to acknowledge,
had found an early fulfillment in the cruel execu-
tion of the Innocents, and the forced exile of Jesus,
Mary and Joseph. Even then the sword of sorrow
had touched her, though this was in sympathy with
others, not for herself. In these instances there was
always the presence of her Child to reassure her, to
calm her fears, to alleviate her anxieties.

The three days of sorrowing when He was lost
were different. Mary and Joseph went from one
travelling group of pilgrims to another, seeking
Him first among their friends and relatives, who
had come up with them and were now returning.
Then followed those harrowing days and nights as

they went from door to door, from place to place in and about Jerusalem, wherever they thought He might be. Yes, this was a new sorrow, something quite different, for His presence was no longer with them—that presence and love which had carried them through some very anxious times.

In spite of who He was, Jesus must have been, up to this time, a very natural boy, because they were looking in all the wrong places for Him! That is to say, they sought Him in all the most *natural* places that a mother would look for a lost child. Where would you expect to find a lost boy of twelve? In the haunts of other boys, the playgrounds, the houses where favorite relatives lived, at the Gates of the City where there were many new and wonderful things to see; probably at the Roman barracks or the court of Herod Antipas where there would be town-boys to show Him the changing of the guard. Apparently Mary and Joseph looked in all these places, as being the most likely, for it took them three days to exhaust the possibilities of where a boy was likely to lose himself; and Jerusalem was not so large. As a last resort, as if it were the last place to find their Boy (and would we not have done the same?), they returned to the Holy Temple!

What a strange sight meets their eyes when, at last, they see Him! The country carpenter and Mary find their Boy sitting in the position of distinction among the learned Doctors of the Law, those of the renowned school of Jewish culture in the Holy City! The Spirit of Wisdom seems to be sitting upon Him. Sorrow and anxiety give place to astonishment and bewilderment as to what He can be doing in such a distinguished circle of men: "And all who were listening to him were amazed at his understanding and his answers. And when they saw him, they were astonished. And his mother said to him, 'Son, why hast thou done so to us? Behold, thy father and I have been seeking thee sorrowing'" (Luke, ii. 48).

The harrowing experiences of loss overflow in these words; they crowd out for the moment the sense of joy and happy relief; even the pride that made itself felt later, of finding Him so well received by these learned men, can find no room for the moment in this Mother's heart. The measure of this sorrow is the measure of love which has been so sorely tried; the sense of responsibility for One who had been given to her by God Himself burdens her soul.

But Jesus reminds His Mother, as many another child has had to do, that He is now grown up. "How is it that you sought me? Did you not know that I must be about my father's business?" (Luke, ii. 49).

Here, for the first time, Jesus speaks to us through the words to His Mother. For the first time He reminds her (for she has grown so used to His human presence) of His Divine mission, of His true Father.

Jesus is reminding Mary that He is not as the rest of men; He has a definite duty to fulfill towards His Eternal Father, and if He does not refer to the sorrow He has caused His Mother, it is because He knows that the fulfillment of the Father's will must, in due time, demand even greater sacrifice of her who loves Him so much. Nevertheless, Jesus returns with them on their journey to Nazareth, "and was subject to them; and his mother [once again] kept all these things carefully in her heart" (Luke, ii. 51).

Here, more than in any other place in the Holy
Gospels, the Holy Spirit of God, through the actions and words of Jesus, shows us the inevitable
pattern which follows upon the giving and accepting of a vocation from God. There is the strife
between nature and super-nature. Even in one so
perfectly attuned as Mary to the will of God,
human love has to combat and be conquered by
that which is divine. Human love cannot see that
present loss may be future gain, and in a much
higher sphere. Jesus showed His Mother that the
Father's will must always come first. But by His
submission to further obedience, He showed that
this can be done without doing violence to the affections and duties which we owe to those in whose
hands God has placed us.

By the sorrows of temporary loss, and the later
joys which followed Jesus' reunion, the Holy Spirit
guided Mary, and she advanced one more step towards the goal which He had in mind for her as
the Mother of our Savior. We see, in one swift
glance, the tremendous change that this episode
wrought in Mary; a change which began when
Jesus declared for the first time in the Temple His

Sonship with the Father. A new relationship comes to Mary as "she pondered these things in her heart." When Jesus again appears in public in the company of Mary His Mother, both have grown—He in favor with God and men, she in spiritual understanding. Now she can say, in the strength and assurance she has learned from the Holy Ghost: "Do whatever he tells you." And through her intervention at Cana of Galilee "he manifested his glory, and his disciples believed in him" (John, ii. 11).

# XVIII

# The Uncalled Witness

*I am alive and was dead, and behold, I am living forever and ever (Apoc., i. 18).*

It is certainly disconcerting to those who wish to follow the footsteps of the Mother of Jesus through the pages of the Gospels, to find an almost complete silence about her during the days of the Resurrection. We must not be disturbed at this, for, as St. John tells us, the Gospels are only a bare outline of the sayings and the works of our Divine Savior. Indeed, we should be most grateful that we have so many revealing facts concerning the Virgin of Nazareth, since the four Evangelists are not writing a "Life of Christ," but only a record of the proof of His Divine Mission and His Divine Person: "There are, however, many other things that Jesus did; but if every one of these should be written, not even the world itself, I think, could hold the books that would have to be written," says

St. John, (xxi. 25). Luke, who writes at greater
length than any of the other sacred writers about
the Mother of God, uses only the intimate secrets
she alone could give him, to the greater purpose of
magnifying her Son.

We must remember that the Resurrection was
to be the central proof of Christ's Divinity; that is
clear from His own reference to it as a sign, given
to the Doctors of the Law, of His rights to preach
the Kingdom of God. It is clearly understood in
this significance by the rulers of the Jews, for they
take every precaution against any liklihood of de-
ception in the matter, placing their own chosen
guards over the tomb; and when, by His own power
Christ is risen in spite of them, the rulers bribe their
guards to lie about the manner of the Resurrection.

Hence, the Evangelists are absorbed in giving
every possible proof of the truth of this great Mystery. They are chiefly concerned in bringing forth
the witnesses to the fact that Christ lived in their
midst for forty days after He had risen from the
dead. In choosing their witnesses, they are careful
to show how each was at first doubtful, and, then,
how they were overwhelmed by the reality of

Christ's return, fully manifesting His Divinty by the fact of rising, fully manifesting His continued humanity by eating and talking with them.

From the point of view, then, of a witness, that is from the viewpoint of the Evangelists, Mary would have been a very poor witness—at least, for those who were unwilling to believe, or who had any suspicions of the truth of the matter. We say this because Mary was in the unique position of having no doubts in the matter, and fully believed in the Resurrection of her Son *before* it came about. Such an attitude might prejudice her in the eyes of those who would consider this a cause of bias. Our Lady did not merely trust and hope that it would be so, as St. John may have done; she fully believed that it would be as He had foretold. In this sense she would not have been a good witness of the event, as an event, because others might suggest that her previous conviction that the Resurrection would take place biased her judgment in the matter. Whereas, the other witnesses were prejudiced *against* the fact, then *later* convinced by the facts which followed. Again, the very fact that Mary was the Mother of Jesus, might well prejudice her as a witness in the eyes of those who were seeking proof. They might say that the sorrow of the mother, her profound love, gave her the illusion that He had risen from the dead. For these reasons, then, if for no others, the Evangelists thought fit not to call her as a witness to her Son's Resurrection.

The Holy Spirit of God revealed to Mary at the Conception that her Son would rule the House of Jacob forever; the same Spirit showed her, as we have seen, how He would be rejected by some, and that her own heart would be pierced by sorrow. In the light of these revelations, and further enlightenment of her soul through grace which has not been made known to us, she witnessed the harrowing drama of the Passion. Her sorrow was not less because she knew that all this shame and disillusionment of the disciples would be dispelled by her Son's triumph over death. Mary's conviction of His coming glory, that it was expedient that He should suffer and so enter into His glory (Luke xxiv. 26), could not, however strong it was, alleviate the pain caused by that suffering on the Cross, and the mystery of His sacrifice for sin. It was in this way that the Holy Spirit had foretold, many years before, that a sword would pierce her heart. It was in this affinity of suffering that she, too, was to enter into the glorious Mystery of the Resurrection, its joys and its peace, its reconciliation of nature and the supernatural, of sin and redemption.

We have been, particularly and intentionally, attentive in these considerations of the Mother of God to the influence of the Divine Spirit in the formation of her spiritual life, and also in the vocation to which He called her. We have seen how gradual that process of embracing her whole life was; how the Spirit of Love leads her step by step to a greater and greater participation in the fullness of the life and purposes of her Son's mission on earth. We have noticed that sudden change, sudden that is to us, from wondering and pondering upon the mysteries hinted at by the Holy Spirit through the words and actions of others, to that moment when Mary, full now of knowledge and faith in the Divine Person of her Son, instigates the first miracle performed by Him in public, which leads to the greater conviction of His disciples. Here, indeed, is an astounding growth in the power of the Holy

Spirit. Whereas all the others surrounding Christ and most of all, His kinsfolk, take all the years up to the Resurrection itself to have this faith in Him, Mary gives evidence of it on the very opening of His public life. It is a change which manifests both the growing power of the Holy Spirit, and the place that Mary was to take at the side of her Son in the future.

In the Mysteries which follow upon the Resurrection we shall be considering yet another great advance of Mary in the power of the Spirit of God. For the days of the Resurrection were largely given over to preparation by the Risen Christ of that intimate band which was to lay the foundations of His universal kingdom on earth; and among those, in a preëminent place, was His Mother. We shall see how the promise of the coming of a new Paraclete, given before and after the Resurrection, was to affect and almost wholly change the position and place of Mary in the great Mystery of the Mystical Body of Christ.

# XIX

## The Days Between

*I will not leave you orphans (John, xiv. 18).*

There are few more striking contrasts recorded
in the Holy Gospels than the two leave-takings of
Jesus—the one before His Sacred Passion, and that
of His Ascension into Heaven.

The Supper Feast of the Passover, usually a joyous feast, is full of forebodings. However explicit
Christ is in His assurances that the Apostles will see
Him again, there is still the fear and dread of His
departure from them; though they have no real
inkling of the manner of His going, they feel the
shadow of death cast across their company. The
promises He makes of returning to them have little
effect upon the sadness that overshadows them.
"Amen, amen, I say to you, that you shall weep and
lament, but the world shall rejoice; and you shall
be sorrowful, but your sorrow shall be turned into
joy. A woman about to give birth has sorrow, be-

cause her hour has come. But when she has brought forth the child, she no longer remembers the anguish for her joy that a man is born into the world. And you therefore have sorrow now; but I will see you again, and your heart shall rejoice, and your joy no one shall take from you" (John, xvi. 20 sq.).

Even such loving words as these make little impression on the disciples. Nor was the promise of another Comforter, the Paraclete, any more effective in removing the apprehension at the thought of their loss.

Contrast the picture which St. John draws for us in his sixteenth chapter with the few pregnant words used by St. Luke to describe Christ's final departure from them at the Ascension: "Now he led them out towards Bethany, and he lifted up his hands and blessed them. And it came to pass as he blessed them, that he parted from them and was carried up into heaven. And they worshipped him, and returned to Jerusalem with great joy. And they were continually in the temple, praising and blessing God" (Luke, xxiv. 50).

It was the joy He had promised them at the Last Supper, a joy which "no one can take from you."

Though the departure of the Divine Master at the Ascension was to be final and complete, in the sense that He would no longer physically walk and talk with them, yet *this* discontinuance of His presence causes no sense of sadness, no apprehension about their future, no loss of confidence in their position as His disciples; on the contrary, they are full of joy. Only one explanation can cover this dramatic change—we may even say, this rather unnatural attitude of theirs. It is because the wonders of the Resurrection, and the intimate instructions Christ has given them during the forty days when He walked again with them, have at last made them realize, and made them realize in an amazingly vivid way, the meaning of the words He spoke to them on that last night before He suffered: "But I speak the truth to you; it is expedient for you that I depart. For if I do not go, the Advocate will not come to you; but if I go, I will send him to you . . . But when he, the Spirit of truth, has come, he will teach you all the truth" (John, xvi. 7, 13).

During the tragedy of the Passion, the idea of any other Comforter was foreign to them; they could not, then, absorb the meaning of Christ when He told them He would send from the Father One who would take His place and have as great an influence upon their lives as He Himself had done. The One whom He would send would be distinct in person, the Spirit of Love, and yet identical in nature.

At the Ascension the words, "I am with you all days even to the consummation of the world" (Matt., xxviii. 20), had a real meaning for Christ's disciples; they had recognized Christ's unity with the Father at the Last Supper: "I came forth from the Father and have come into the world. Again I leave the world and go to the Father." Hereupon His disciples said to Him: "Behold, now thou speakest plainly, and utterest no parable. Now we know that thou knowest all things, and dost not need that anyone should question thee. For this reason we believe that thou camest forth from God" (John, xvi. 28 sq.).

Now, through His instructions during the "forty days," they come to recognize the significance of His abiding presence through the Spirit of Love, who would come in a special manner and abide with them all days; and with the Spirit would be the glorious Christ, the Head of the Mystical Body, His Church. Until the Holy Spirit came in His fullness, they may show signs of fear of men, but there was nothing but spiritual joy in the glory of the Ascension; all were now animated with that spirit which caused Peter to exclaim on Tabor at Christ's Transfiguration and anticipation of the Ascension: "Master, it is good for us to be here" (Luke, ix. 33).

It would be impossible, either in our own minds or in fact, to dissociate the Mother of God from this new atmosphere of spiritual joy which animated the disciples.

For Mary the Ascension was the culmination of her Son's life, of that human life of which she had been the human agent. The sorrows and the anxieties of the Mother of God, which were very real but unable to dim the faith and hope she always had in His triumph, were now a thing of the past. The Holy Virgin entered into those forty days with the Risen Christ with a far greater anticipation than the disciples, to whom the Resurrection came in some manner of a surprise. The spiritual balance, which we have again and again remarked in the character of the Blessed Mother, did not, as in the case of the Apostles, cause her to sway from a state of spiritual desolation to one of extreme expectancy. The Apostles, in their new-found joy, pressed Jesus for an answer to the question ever uppermost in their minds, and which they had asked Him before the Passion: "Lord, wilt thou at this time restore the kingdom to Israel?" Mary knew that the Kingdom of which He had preached, and for which He had died, was not the Kingdom that the Apostles had in mind.

The Ascension of Christ, and the particular promises He had then made, did give to the Mother of Jesus a new expectancy; but it was the anticipation of the power and life which would come with the new Comforter Jesus had promised to send. Mary, much more than any other intimates of Jesus, knew from joyous experience a great deal of the power and life of that Holy Spirit of Divine Love. He it was who had taken her as His Spouse; He it was who had given her all the joy of her unexpected motherhood; He it was who had given her the Divine Child, Jesus. Now, He was to come in another manner; there was to be another overshadowing of the Holy Spirit. He could not give her back her Son in the manner He had given Him in the first place; but the new Annunciation would mean, Mary knew, something equally wonderful— another manifestation of God's love for men, a new birth, the Conception of the Mystical Body of Christ.

# XX

## *Counsel of the Fishermen*

*She reacheth therefore from end to end mightily, and ordereth all things sweetly (Wis., viii. 1).*

Biologists and biographers may resent the statement that they have something in common. Yet, if we consider the motives by which they are urged to undertake their studies and work, and the main objectives of their researches and writings, we will see that there is more than an accidental kinship in their professions.

The biologists would be the first to admit that they have an innate curiosity about the origin, the laws of development and growth of plants and animals. They would admit that their chief contribution to science is to set out in order how these things came to be, what is the relationship between this family and that, to give to the world a picture of "life" in a particular branch, or a general review of the plant and animal kingdoms. The biologist

loves to unfold for us the secret forces which under-
lie that great world of plants and animals we so
casually take for granted.

The biographer is a specialist, in the sense that
he takes an individual, a human being, and gives us
a review of his life. What is it that causes the writer
to spend years gathering together data about an
individual, except that he and his reading public
have a profound curiosity about the origins of this
or that man's success or failure in life?

To satisfy this curiosity the biographer sets out
in order the human relationships between his subject and the human and material instruments which
made the individual stand out among his fellows.

Scientist and writer have this common trait of
curiosity, each, in his own field, is interested in re-
discovering for himself the whys and wherefores of
things or persons. They are not satisfied with the
outward and superficial explanation given by common observation. Hence, they gather together all
the possible information they can find, co-ordinate
it and then, much to their delight, spring a surprise upon us by their revelations, and astound us
by their theories as to why we have been wrong in

our estimate of certain trends of life, or concerning a certain individual's character.

Biographical writings are popular because they help to satisfy the human demand for knowledge, and they do so in a particular manner. In the biographical sketch we not only add to our knowledge, but we also, in a certain sense, identify ourselves with the characters involved. We are not only curious, but we like to feel that we were right about our estimate of another, or to guess what were the origins of success or failure, and how we would have met those hidden forces. We like to get behind the complexity of an individual's life, which is obvious, to the simple answer which we feel will give us the key to all the unanswered questions concerning him.

What is true in the case of individuals is very often true in the case of organizations. Those who witness to-day the internal unity, the world-wide power and overwhelming political and social strength of the United States can hardly believe the humble origins, and the internal weaknesses out of which power and strength have been wrought. Hundreds of historians have written volumes trying to explain for us how this historical phenomenon has come about; there is something unique in the American character which has brought unity out of such mixed and contradictory characteristics. Where other nations have become great by the purity of their stock, America has become famous by dissimilarity of origins.

It will be obvious that the greater distance in time there is between the origin of a society and its present form, the harder it will be to trace what we now know to its initial causes. So, too, the more widespread and complicated it has become, the less easy it will be to determine its primitive and simple form, namely, what gave it birth.

Of all the institutions, religious, political, and social which have influenced mankind, none has had a wider, more constant and effective part to play upon individuals and other organizations than the Catholic Church. The persecutions and the bitter libels of writers and historians are the most eloquent witnesses of this fact.

A bitter critic of the Church, such as Lord Macaulay, the historian, could not, in all truth, withhold his admiration of the constitution of that

Church which he recognized as the greatest organization in history, and which he predicted would outlive the organized civilization of his own country and the Empire of which he was so proud.

In an age which is seeking world-organization, political, social and economic, men find already existent a religious institution which has every mark of universality in time and place; an institution which is identical in its government, in its teaching, and in its ability to bring happiness to men. This, they find, is true in every age of the Church's history going back over the centuries of our western civilization.

The pomp and circumstance, the tie with every nation, race and culture, the discipline throughout of over three hundred million men and women—all this leaves the inquirer wondering what is the secret of its religious dominance nineteen hundred years after it foundation!

The social-scientist, the historian and the materialistic philosopher have found, each according to his own habits and method, a hundred and one answers to the complex question of the Church's continued power and influence, to its unity and continuity, to its universal appeal and capacity to hold the fidelity of so varied a membership. We know that each one of the answers given us is insufficient in itself, and many of them are contradictory.

As Catholics we know the answer to the question of our Church's continuity in life and influence. We know, because we have within us that "Thing" which first gave the Church life; we feel and know that we are part of that living force which makes the Church One and Universal; we know, because we are members one of another; not merely are we part of those who now live as members of the Church, but one with all those who have gone before us in the sign of the Faith. Further, we know this because we are conscious that we are the living temples of the Holy Spirit of God; and it is that same Spirit who overshadowed that small band of men and women, together with the Mother of Jesus, on the first Pentecost, the Birthday of the Mystical Body of Christ.

Whatever tremendous changes, and they have been many, have taken place in the *outward* form and size, the outward organization and influence of the Mystical Body, have come about by the operation of the Spirit of Truth; nor do these changes puzzle us, as they so seriously confuse others; for we know that it is the same Spirit who worketh all in all.

All the incredible history of the Catholic Church throughout the centuries (and whatsoever shall happen in the future) goes back to that scene in the Cenacle where a band of men was gathered around the Mother of Jesus; here, indeed, is the mystery and the secret of the ever-living Church of God, the Divine Spirit of Love appearing, like "parted tongues as of fire" (Acts, ii. 3).

The Coming Down of the Spirit of God was a new birth, that of the Mystical Body of Christ; and we shall see how the figure of the Virgin, who was overshadowed by the same Spirit that she might be the instrument of our salvation, was, at this second overshadowing, destined to take an equal part in the formation of the Mystical Body of her Son.

From the moment of the wonder of Pentecost the figure of Mary takes a new and striking place in the life of that humble band of men to whom, under God, we owe the Faith we now hold so dear.

# XXI

# *Our Mother Has Gone*

*In all these I sought rest, and I shall abide in the inheritance of the Lord (Ecclus., xxiv. 11).*

There is not one of us, no matter how perfect we may be, who is not apprehensive of death. There are good men and women, who really make their life a preparation for death; they are men and women of real faith, because faith teaches us that this is precisely what life is meant to be. Yet, even with such good people, there is still some fear in their hearts concerning this finality of man. With such as these, it is a mild fear; one of uncertainty as to whether they have made sufficient preparation.

To the majority of men the fear of death is founded in their attachment to the things of this life; whether this is the possession of wealth, the attachment to persons whom they love, or the pride of life—pride in their position of rank or fame. There is little cure for this fear, except the total change of attitude towards one's sense of possession of the things of this world; and that is a great grace.

Nevertheless, in both the good and the less good, we must recognize that the fear of death is partly natural, partly supernatural. Fear of death is natural, because it arises from the sense of evil there is in the fact of death. It is a matter of faith that God made us, in the first instance, with no intention that we should die. Death, which we consider a natural phenomenon in all other living things, was never meant to touch man. That it does, is because it is an imposed penalty. God gave to the first two human beings the gift of immortality. Part of that gift is still the right of man—the immortality of his spirit; it is only his body which receives the penalty of death. But God, who infuses an immortal soul in every man, never intended the soul should be separated from his body, and the latter should see corruption. Death in this sense is, therefore, an evil; we may say an unnatural event, from the viewpoint of God's intentions. Hence, at the thought of death we have the natural reaction of fear.

By a preternatural gift, God intended that the body of man should always be, even in eternity, the temple of the human soul. He wished that the immortal spirit of man, which was made to know, love and serve Him, should always be enshrined in the human body; that the body, which is the instrument through which man's spirit knows his Creator, should share in the reward which would come through following that knowledge with his love. In this sense, all the channels through which man enjoys life would become the means of eternal happiness in body, as well as in soul.

Through divine revelation we know that death has come to man through original sin; it is thus we know that death is a penalty, and not just a natural phenomenon.

The whole doctrine of the Assumption of the Mother of God is based upon the facts of revelation stated above. There is only this to add: since the Mother of God was conceived without original sin, since sin was never in life contracted by her, it would seem repugnant to us to suppose that the penalties of sin were inflicted upon her. As we know by faith that Mary was the one unique creature preserved from the stain of that sin which brought death into the world, so it is through faith we believe that she was preserved from the corruption of the body.

The Eastern Church has a beautiful expression for the passing of the Mother of God from this world, from this valley of tears, to her eternal reward: they call it the "Dormition," the "Falling Asleep" of the Mother of God.

There are, of course, other very solid grounds for our belief in the Assumption of the Mother of God into heaven. Perhaps that which is of most consolation to us, is her union with the Divine Spirit of God. The Incarnate Word of God was conceived by the power of the Holy Ghost, and He sanctified her in preparation for her Motherhood of the Son of God. Thus, this union with the Holy Spirit was unique in kind and character. Mary was the Shrine of God, of the Word made flesh; she was the very Holy of Holies.

If part of *our* reward in heaven will be the reunion of our soul and body at the general resurrection, how much more fitting it is that the Mother of God, from whose flesh the Son of God took His humanity, should receive her immediate reward by being received into the glory which she now has in heaven with the Risen Christ!

When considering the Mystery of the Assumption, we cannot expect fully to enter into the secret of God's ways, but we can ask of the Mother of God that we may, while remaining here below, share to a greater and greater degree in the union with the Holy Spirit of God whom she enshrined. We may ask of her that she will give us the true fear of God, a gift of the same Spirit, whereby divine love enters into our lives banishing the human and natural fear of death.

We can learn from the Spirit of Truth how to use earthly talents and gifts of body so as to make this necessary mortal partner of our lives the instrument of our sanctification. It was God's will that we should be one being who would know, love and serve Him. It is His will now, and for this has He sent His Divine Spirit into the world to restore all things in Christ Jesus.

May He, through the intercession of the Mother of God, restore to us in greater measure union with Him, a union which will place us one day in assurance of glory with her and our full union for eternity with God!

# XXII

# The King's Daughter

*A great sign appeared in heaven: a Woman clothed with the sun (Apoc., xii. 1).*

St. Paul, in one of his great letters to the faithful whom he had converted, warns them concerning too great a curiosity concerning the next life; he does so in these very beautiful words: "Eye has not seen, nor ear heard, nor has it entered into the heart of man what things God has prepared for those who love him" (I Cor., ii. 9). It would seem that the faithful of those early days had started speculating about their future life, so care-free were they about the benefits of this one. St. Paul, to whom many secrets of the hereafter had been revealed, was quite definite that, whatever such speculations were, they would fall far short of the reality and wonder of our reward.

There is no doubt that men and women will go on till the end of time wondering what the reward of virtue will be; and each guess will be as futile as the last. If theologians and preachers, poets and painters, are going to fall so far short of the truth, there is little point in trying to picture to ourselves, in these few considerations, what must have been the final reward of the Mother of God, after her Assumption into Heaven. If in our own case the reward prepared for us is so far beyond our human experience or comprehension, what must it be in regard to the Immaculate Mother?

We shall, therefore, in the last glorious Mystery of the Mother of God, consider something which is nearer our own experience, something which, while mysterious, is partly within our narrow limits of understanding. We have from time to time made mention of the Mystical Body of Christ. This is a doctrine of the Church which is receiving great and wider attention every day. In simple terms the Mystical Body of Christ expresses what is said of the Communion of Saints in our catechism, though it means more than simply a union of the faithful on earth, in purgatory, and in heaven.

Certainly the Mystical Body of Christ means union, it means union of souls through the vivifying

Spirit of God; it is, therefore, a union of Divine Love. It is not just a union of human love, though that love carries on beyond this life. It is a union of grace, won for us through the merits of Christ's Sacrifice, and the inpouring of the Holy Ghost.

If our union with God through grace is secure at the moment of death, then we are certain of eternal union with Him in heaven, though we may have to be cleansed in the love-flames of purgatory. What is also certain is that we shall have eternal union with all those others who have been united with God on earth, and are now united with Him in heaven. Perhaps it is only when we think of this that we understand the insistence of St. John upon the love of one another in Christ while on earth. If the Spirit of Divine Love does not unite us here on earth, if we are not willing to share His Love with others (however humanly trying they may be) while we are on earth, how can we hope to meet them in terms of love in the presence of God Himself? Charity, the most enduring virtue of the Holy Spirit, is the first essential for the attaining of life with God and His Saints in eternity.

It is a sober doctrine of truth that the most casual

meeting of man and man here on earth may be the introduction to an eternal friendship in heaven. We never know how the most ordinary word or deed may be a link and bond of love with that same person for all time, though we met but once on earth. Christ Himself promised us there would be many surprises awaiting us when we came to that life with Him which will be without end. "Lord, when did we see thee hungry, and feed thee; or thirsty, and give thee drink? . . . as long as you did it for one of these, the least of my brethren, you did it for me" (Matt., xxv. 37, 40).

The bond of grace and love which binds the members of the Mystical Body of Christ one to another is, in kind, the same in all; the difference between one and another on earth, as it will be in heaven, is the quality of our union with God. The Mother of God has received the greatest reward in heaven because of the unique union she had with God; she is the Queen of All Saints because of the intimate union they have made with her through the influence of the Spirit of Love; as He enshrined Himself in the heart of Mary, so they have enshrined her image and figure in their hearts. There is not a sinner on earth who could not have shared in that love which the Mother of Christ has for everyone who has been saved by His Precious Blood. As the Mother of Divine Grace, she is ever dispensing the means of saving souls; part of her reward in heaven is to make known to men the Gift of Divine Love in which she shares so fully. Her glory will be that she has ever been the Refuge of Sinners, the Comforter of the Afflicted; her desire is to see that no soul is lost to the membership of the Mystical Body of her Divine Son.

The Mission of the Holy Spirit is to enkindle the fire of love on earth, to bring the ignorant to truth, the unclean to holiness, the imperfect to perfection, the children of Mary and co-heirs of Christ to that union with the Father, and the Son, which was begun in the Holy Spirit while they were yet on earth, but will be without end in heaven.

# XXIII

# Re-Introductions

*She reneweth all things, and through nations conveyeth herself into holy souls (Wis., vii. 27).*

We have seen that the opening page of the history of Our Lord Jesus Christ was marked by the overshadowing of the Spirit of God. To the Holy Ghost is attributed the first act of the Mystery of the Incarnation. So too, in the formation of the Mystical Body of Christ, which is His Church, do we have the recording of the second overshadowing of the Spirit of Love and Wisdom—on that great day of Pentecost when the Virgin took upon herself a new place and office, and the Apostles truly entered into their labors.

We have noted also the significance that in both of these instances, which meant so much to the human race, Mary the Virgin of Nazareth had a very definite place. In the first, she was chosen as the Mother of God, than which there could be no greater favor given to a human being. In this great office of motherhood she had the most intimate concern with the Mystery of our Redemption. In the second instance, all we are told is that the Mother of Jesus was present on Pentecost. It is tradition, the history and records of others' lives, which shows us the subsequent position and influence which the Mother of God has had in the Mystical Body of Christ; it is this tradition which shows us that her place there on Pentecost was of equal, if very different, importance as in the first overshadowing at the Conception of the Incarnate Word.

The life of the Mother of God, both in its manifestation in the Holy Gospels and still more in the life within the Communion of Saints, has always been a treasury of meditations for those who would advance towards a closer relationship with her Son. Her holiness was not only unique in regard to her preservation from original sin, but has been and will ever remain a pattern for those who ponder upon the mysteries of active grace. She is the supreme example of those who have been daily guided by the Holy Spirit of God, of those who have wrought great things by grace amidst the routine and background of everyday life.

Those who at any time wish to consider closely the influence of the Spirit of God, the work of the Paraclete, can do no better than meditate upon Mary, the Immaculate Spouse of the Holy Ghost, in whom His grace was never wanting, and who corresponded so fully with His divine inspirations.

It is hard, without the practical example given us by the Virgin Mary, to comprehend the purpose and influences of His Seven Gifts, which we have seen had such an active and practical bearing upon Mary's life. In the other Saints of God we see these same Gifts, and their influence upon human actions and vocations, but we see them in different degrees of perfection. Sometimes the Holy Spirit withdraws a chosen soul from the world, and then His influence is largely manifested in the contemplative life. At another time the influence of the Holy Spirit upon a man or woman is manifested in the wonders wrought through these Saints in the active world, in the apostolate of Christ; again, perhaps, the influence is manifested in circumstances which have very little likeness or af-

finity to our own lives whether in the home or
the cloister.

In Mary, we shall find the work of the Holy
Spirit both in the sphere which we call contemplative, and in that which we call active. We shall see,
if we look closely into her life, how the Spirit influenced a Mother and a Virgin; one who had, and
fulfilled, all the duties and obligations of Motherhood, whether in the home or among neighbors;
one who, at the same time, remained the Ever Virgin Mary, the Handmaid of the Lord. Further, it
is quite clear from the history of the Saints that
Mary has not been wanting in her part in that
work which we call apostolic, the growth of the
Mystical Body of Christ her Son.

Here, in these thoughts we shall try to transfer
our knowledge of the Holy Spirit of God to the
character and example of the Mirror of Justice;
and so perhaps more readily understand, in a practical manner, what should be His mission within our
own souls. At the same time, as we contemplate
the indwelling of the Holy Spirit in Mary, we shall
see how His holy operation is to affect our lives.

The Mother of God has, if we may use the picturesque phrase, been walking down the arches of the years dispensing to us the Gifts of the Holy Spirit of God. It would be very hard indeed to pick upon any one Saint of God in whom we shall not find the influence of the Mother of Jesus. These men and women, of every race and age, have somehow found in her the necessary support and strength which they needed daily to carry the Cross of her Divine Son. From her they received much of that inspiration without which it is impossible long to continue in the spiritual life. It is these same men and women of everyday life who have handed down to us century by century the Catholic love of the Mother of God. If many words were not written concerning her in the history of her Son, her life is written deep in the hearts and minds of all those whom she has not disdained to call her children.

The mission of Mary among the sons and daughters of the Eternal Father has frequently been manifested in startling ways, but very much more frequently it has only been known to those who have worshipped at some lonely shrine, where she introduced them to the Spirit of Love, the Comforter to help and assist them on their way.

# XXIV

## All-Glorious Within

*As the lily among thorns, so is my love among the daughters (Cant., ii. 2).*

It was Christ who told us that the Spirit breathes where He will. Souls are chosen without regard to rank, class or color, divisions made by men of the world. Some of His chosen disciples are to be found in the cloisters of religious, some in the priesthood, most of them in the work-a-day world around us. We may rub shoulders in the subways, in our workshop, in the schoolroom, with those who have a special call from God to give themselves in a particular way to Him; His secret is theirs, and we may never share in it, or even guess that they are so close to God.

Those who have been given a special vocation by the Spirit of God were not chosen because of any special gifts in the human sense; not always because they had any special leanings towards religion as children. His choice must ever remain a mystery of divine grace, a matter of profound humility and thanksgiving for those whom He calls to become Temples of the Holy Ghost.

We have seen how He comes to them, first of all in that solemn dedication of Baptism—with His inpouring of the gifts of faith, hope and charity, that they may first see, desire, and be united to the Godhead, of which He is the Spirit of Love. Thus is the first marriage-bond of grace made between God and a chosen soul. Later, when these three graces have had their influence upon the initial stages of life, we have seen that He comes to them again, bringing His sevenfold treasure of the Gifts of Confirmation. Such is the rebirth of every man and woman who wishes to enter into the union of the Sonship of God through Jesus Christ.

If we except the wonderful privilege of the preservation of Our Lady from original sin (a grace given solely on account of her office as the Mother of God), then the spirituality of Mary was not different in kind from our own. The choice made in this instance by the Spirit of God was, from a human standpoint, as mysterious as any call of His to a human creature. To none was the choice more astounding than to the Virgin of Nazareth: "How shall this be done?" If a choice for the dignity of being made the Mother of the Savior had been left in the hands of men, how different that choice would have been! We can imagine the pomp and circumstance there would have been in making the selection, the multitude of conditions, the necessary qualifications that would have been demanded of one to be chosen for this honor. Yet, whatever that choice might have been, we know that with all the care taken she would never have met with the requirements fit for such a position: ultimately, it was God alone who could make the preparation for a vocation so unique.

In spite of the fact that Mary's call by God was to be so much higher than that of any other creature, the circumstances in which she had to follow the call were, if anything, more commonplace than those of most of the men and women whom we now call Saints. Mary, more than any of the chosen of God before and after her, could truly say her life was hidden in God. Rather could we say it was hidden *with* God; because for thirty years she had to care and work for One who was in all reality the very Son of God. Still, though her life was hidden thus with God, it was not hidden in the cloisters of a religious house; it was hidden within the walls of a cottage in the village of Nazareth; her life was hidden beneath the duties of a mother, the anxieties of a poor and hardworking housekeeper.

It was thus for thirty years that Mary enshrined the Spirit of God; only once or twice during those years was there to be anything exceptional in her life; only once or twice was the divine life to shine through the human and humbler mode of her living. Though no creature was to come so close to the Three Divine Persons, and have a more intimate concern for the Incarnate Word, who Himself put aside His divine glory and took the form of a servant; yet, who was more familiar with the ordinary things of life than Our Lady—its joys and sorrows, its daily duties and obligations, its trials and small triumphs?

If we are to judge by the fruits of the Spirit, we must conclude that it was in this very conformity of her life with the daily duties it brought, that the

Spirit of God found a correspondence unequalled by any of the Saints whom the Holy Ghost has sanctified. She, the simple Virgin of Nazareth, is now known as the Queen of Confessors and Virgins, the Queen of All Saints! She has become the Mirror of Justice, the Justice after which the Saints hungered; in her they have found the reflection of those virtues and graces with which they have wished to adorn their souls.

There is no branch of activity within the Mystical Body of Christ, whether it be organized by men or women, which has not taken the lonely Virgin Mary as its patroness. This is not only because of her great dignity as the Mother of Jesus, but because they have found within the narrow limits of their lives a kinship with the circumstances of her life, and they have seen how God has chosen the frail things of this life to manifest His power, the lowly things to confound the proud.

The humble stock from which we come, the ordinariness of our lives, should not deter us from answering the call of the Holy Spirit of God. It may be that we have allowed the everyday affairs of life to crowd out and still the voice of the Spirit within us. Better that we should ponder and bear the mysteries of His grace in our hearts, that we may in due time manifest His power, and bear the fruits of His indwelling.

# XXV

# *Kinship*

*In me is all the grace of the way (Ecclus., xxiv. 25).*

The first recorded tribute to Our Lady was that
of the Archangel Gabriel, when he greeted the future Mother of God, not by her own name, but by
a title of singular beauty: "Hail, full of grace." It
was a title which most fittingly expressed the chief
characteristic of Mary, her holiness.

Holiness, living life with grace, was indeed a
birthright for Mary, because she was conceived
without sin. In this does she differ from us all, who
begin life in separation from God. But, as we have
said, that life of grace was not different in kind,
only in degree, from our own vital contact with
God, whereby we are made sons of God. Supernaturally her life was much fuller, more constant,
more part of herself. So true is this that tradition
and love of men through the centuries have given
her another title, and called her "Spiritual Vessel,"

as if the retaining and preservation of grace were the purpose of her life. And who shall doubt it?

Fuller, indeed, was that life with grace, but in kind the same as ours. Thus, in so far as we live by grace, we have a source of likeness to Mary; for we are the children of the Mother of Grace, bearing in our souls the image of her Divine Son, if so it be that the Spirit of God dwells within us. Those, therefore, who have made it their aim in life to imitate the Holy Virgin, to take her as their model and ideal, to try and make their humble lives akin to hers, are not trifling with some vague and unreal mode of living; they are trying to increase in the greatest reality of all, the grace of God. This participation in the divine nature has its own laws, its own God-given powers, its own form of beauty; and the Saints have approached this holiness of life through the most perfect Mirror of Justice, knowing that in their imitation of Mary they will come ever nearer to the holiness to which they are called in knowing, loving and serving God.

Holiness in Mary drew all its strength and constancy from the abiding presence of the Holy Spirit. That habit of hers, to which we have so often referred, of keeping and pondering all things in her heart, shows how much she depended on the supernatural for her interpretation of what God's will might be, and for the inspiration to fulfill it.

If we think for a moment of how dependent we are upon our senses of touch, sight and hearing for our contact with our fellow-men, so that our life is wholly stunted with the loss of even one of these channels of communication, we shall realize how dependent we are in the matter of knowledge and love of others upon these instruments of communication. We have seen that there are in our soul "senses," instruments of communication which have much the same purpose, in the spiritual order, as our outward senses have in the natural order. By these we hear the counsels of the Holy Ghost, by them we are sensitive to the influence of active grace on the one hand, and to anything approaching evil on the other. By them we follow the Will of God within and without us.

The spirituality, the holiness, of Mary was essentially based on the exercise of these spiritual qualities of the soul, which, we have seen, are the Gifts of the Holy Ghost. Tradition has given the title of "Holy" to Mary; this is only another way of expressing the working of the Holy Spirit of God. For it is only by the fact that the Holy Spirit guides us in all truth that we can be certain that our imitation of the Mother of God is what He wishes of us, namely, to imitate her virtues. Tradition, guided by the Holy Spirit of God, has made Mary the model of all the virtues, because we are more readily drawn to one who showed herself perfectly human in all her actions, and yet remained so close to God. We have seen how each of the Gifts of the Holy Spirit played its part in the development of her spiritual character; it is the perfection of the work of these Gifts which has drawn all men and women to acclaim her holiness by the prayers and hymns of the faithful throughout the ages.

What does it matter if the outward circumstances of our lives are so different from those which shaped the earthly life of the Mother of God, if the same Divine Spirit who overshadowed her is the source of life which is centered in the mind and heart of men? Time and space give way to the power of the spirit, which knows no such limitations. Spirituality, after all, is concerned with eternity, with the

143

eternal love of God, with our eternal union with God by grace. Our kinship with the Mother of God is in and through the Spirit of God; she can help us most in our small endeavor to become like her, a vessel of God's election, because she has been so closely associated with the Son of God in our salvation. Her intimate concern that we should seek her patronage is illustrated in the many personal interventions she has made in the lives of the Saints, and in the Orders of which she has been the inspiration. When we lift up our hearts in prayer during the Litany of the Mother of God, we are but following the spontaneous appeal of those thousands and thousands of men and women in the past who have given her those beautiful titles, and who have come to a deeper understanding of the ways of God through her tuition and help.

The "Spiritual Vessel" is overflowing with that love which we can only hope to retain by faithfulness to the Spirit of Love and Wisdom, who gave Mary to us to be our Advocate and the Mother of All Grace.

## XXVI

# Mother of the Living

*O Fairest among women! (Cant., i. 7).*

All through the Books of the Old Testament, and indeed in many of the poems of the ancient pagan writers there is to be found a common theme concerning the make-up of man. Philosophers and poets of the far-off days were often agreed that man was in some way misshapen, that there was a source of conflict within him for which it was hard to account. There arose a theory among the ancients that there had been a "golden age," in which man lived in happiness without doing violence to his fellows, in which his highest ideals were fulfilled, in which there was true conformity between what he desired and what he attained. Some of these myths and poems came very near to the truth of the matter, not perhaps in the details, but in the substance of their message to men.

The Old Testament was more definite; in fact,

it reveals to us the truth concerning what we now so well know as the fall of man. Only the revelation of God could convey to us the truth that mankind was destined to a supernatural state of life, and from this he fell, and as a consequence there has ever remained a conflict between his purposes in life.

It is the New Testament, the Revelation of the Son of God, which makes known to us the restoration of mankind to the high destiny for which, in primitive times, he proved himself unworthy. It is the same revelation of God which shows us the manner of this restoration—through the Sacrifice of Christ and sanctification by the Holy Spirit of God.

Further, we know from the same sacred writing of Scripture that there was one creature of God, a woman, who escaped the penalty of man's fall from grace, a woman who was destined to be the Mother of God. When considering the holiness of Our Lady it is essential to keep in mind the fact, which has its basis in her Immaculate Conception, that the Holy Spirit found in her the unique child of God.

When the Holy Ghost comes to us, first in Baptism and later in a special manner in Confirmation, He has first of all a work of reformation to perform in the soul of man. He has to rectify habits and tendencies of mind and will. These are often flesh-bound, and tending to a life lower in standard than the supernatural to which man is called. The Holy Spirit finds at His approach a person already self-determined, one already attentive to the attractions and pleasures natural to his earthly state of life. Indeed, the Holy Ghost comes when we are first awakening to what life can give us. He comes when we are first realizing life's possibilities, when we are absorbed in that period of preparation for what is yet to come to us by a hundred and one different channels. That is the first work of the Holy Spirit, to rectify in us what has a wrong tendency. Gently, He forces us to listen to Him within, when there is so much else to engage our attention without. He has to make our souls sensitive to His presence when we are so conscious of things around us, and of new forces within us.

In Mary, the Holy Spirit found a soul that had known and fully realized its supernatural life from the dawn of reason. Mary never had any tendencies which were not in perfect harmony with the Divine Will. She never had any habits of mind or will which would have caused her to act apart from, or independent of, God. Therefore, the Holy Spirit had in no sense to adjust her outlook on life. He never had to elevate anew her aspirations, nor detach her from what we would call worldliness. The Holy Spirit's first work in Mary began at a stage in her spiritual development the counterpart of which, in us, is near perfection. His work was complete possession, complete union, complete and uncontested victory. This was because she had never contracted original sin, because from the first moment of her existence the Holy Spirit informed her soul, filling it with His grace and gifts.

We have seen how the faith of the Mother of God was transformed by this unimpeded union with God; how unhesitating were her actions because of the close guidance of the Spirit of Truth; how the external obstacles of her life, placed there by human failure, were overcome by the Gift of Fortitude; how fear was not a means of keeping her from evil, so much as an impulse that attracted her to God. All of these indications of spiritual perfection owe their origin to her unique union with God from the moment when He gave her life.

Such a consideration of the union of the Mother of God and the Holy Spirit may give us a feeling —it is nothing more—that Our Lady is very far removed from our sphere of spirituality and experience of the presence of God. That is not just, nor is it a profitable attitude. It gives us only an excuse for our own shortcomings. This relationship between Mary and the Paraclete should draw us nearer, not further from her.

If the Mirror of Justice dazzles us, if we think of her as someone wholly apart from ourselves, we should reflect a little more deeply. In the realm of created things—the perfect order of the seasons, the constant reproduction of life in all its kingdoms, the concord in the heavens above, and the teeming life in the waters below—in all these spheres the exception that startles us is the failure of any one thing issuing from the hand of God to fulfill His will. It puzzles us to know how a created thing can fail, of its kind, to be perfect, considering the origin of its creation.

Surely, it is far more astounding, a terrible reflection to have to make, that man, the one intelligent being, the constituted lord of nature, has alone caused chaos in this world! The general rule for man is that he more consistently frustrates God's law than he fulfills it!

The one perfect exception is the Mother of God. She throughout her life never failed God. In her we see the perfect example of all that grace can achieve where it is not impeded by sin, and especially by the effects of original sin. Had we not inherited the sin of Adam, we would have come closer to that constant perfection found in the soul of Mary.

Far from regarding Mary as one afar off, we should desire to have her in our midst. By faltering steps we can still fulfill the Will of God. This we will do by seeking that perfection found in the Immaculate Virgin; though not espoused to the Spirit of Love as she was, yet we will be united by the bonds of grace, and find kinship with her whom we call our Mother.

## XXVII

# Reflections in a Mirror

*The unspotted Mirror of God's Majesty (Wis., vii. 26).*

However great the development of Christian doctrine may be, whether in the past or in the future, it is certain that tradition never departs from the primary laws set by the revelation of Christ. We have seen that Christ Himself promised and after His Ascension sent the Holy Spirit of Truth that His Church might never fail. Human tradition can and does fail; for this reason Christ guarded against this threatening error by giving us the Holy Spirit.

There are those who have taught that many of the outward changes which they see to-day in the Church of God, and which were certainly not there in the times of the Apostles, are erroneous teachings, rites and ceremonies which have received the sanction of human tradition, but are contrary to the revelation of God.

We know from the words of Christ, from His parable of the mustard tree, that His Church is to have abundant life. Christ, then, accounted for that change which comes with every form of life. If the things we are concerned with in the growth of His Church come from within, and are not mere accidental additions, these changes must come from that life of the Church which is the Holy Spirit of God. Anything, therefore, which appertains to the traditional teaching of the Church as such, must have had its roots in the seedlings of the revealed words of the Son of God. We must also remember that, as St. John tells us, Christ revealed many things concerning the Kingdom of God which are not written in the New Testament.

All that we have said in summary, has special reference to the devotion of the faithful to the Mother of God. There seems to be a lack of proportion between the devotion to Mary in Apostolic times and in our own days. All that we know of our Blessed Lady is to be found in two places, Scripture and Catholic Tradition. Concerning the latter, her position is best summed up in that title we have already mentioned, the Mirror of Justice.

If we contemplate the Mother of God in the framework of Scripture, we do not find our thoughts center wholly upon her. On the contrary, even in the intimate center of her life given us by St. Luke, her soul truly magnifies and enlarges our knowledge of God. All the solemnity of the Annunciation, which so closely concerned the motherhood of Mary, reflects the divine mission of her Son rather than her own interests; shows forth the will of God in our regard as much as it shows the delicate submission of Mary to that will.

It is characteristic of small souls that they are essentially self-centered. They attract or attempt to attract everything—by their conversations, their actions—to themselves. Mary by every thought, word and deed showed that she was the mirror of selflessness. Her will reflected not her own whims and desires; it reflected the will of God: "Be it done to me according to thy word" (Luke, i. 38). Her mind was not centered upon herself, but upon the great things that God had done in her regard and ours. It is noteworthy that the greatest and most intimate self-revelation of the mind and heart of Our Lady is her *Magnificat*. This is a poem in which is mirrored, in inspired words, the work of God our Savior, His power and majesty. That is the greatness and the office of the Mother of God—to magnify and mirror the justice and glory of God.

Catholic tradition makes clearer the public position of Mary. The Litany of Loreto, which is a summary of the titles given her by tradition, is a hymn of praise to her, but equally it is one to God Himself. In the Mirror of Justice we see the Mother of God reflected under different forms and titles. But, these mirrored forms, like the historic person of Mary, do not hold our whole attention. They cause the mind to pass on and to pierce the divine light surrounding them. It is the special purpose of a mirror to reflect something greater than itself—a light of greater wonder, things beyond the native vision. Meditation upon the different aspects of the Virgin's life enables us to do this, too, in relation to God. We see in Mary the Mirror of Justice, the Star of the Sea, but she reflects not her own light but the "Light of the Gentiles and the Glory of thy people Israel" (Luke, ii. 32). We may see there the "Ark of the Covenant," but, at the same time, we are forced to consider the Lamb of God who taketh away the sins of the world, and who sealed that Covenant with His own Precious Blood. We may find in that Mirror "Mary the Gate of Heaven," and we are carried through her to the very throne of God.

If Mary is the Mirror of Justice, in the sense that she always reflects the Divine Presence, she has also the power to show us our own dwarfed spirituality. What is more important, meditation upon the attributes and graces of the Mother of God shows us the gigantic possibilities of a soul courageous enough to attempt to make real in its own sanctuary the forms reflected in the soul of Mary.

Thus it is that both in her life with us on earth and in the figure of this holy Virgin which has been handed down to us from generation to generation, there is the same substantial holiness of grace; the forms of devotion and imitation given to her may change, but the reason is the same to-day as it was at the moment when the Archangel paid her the compliment of calling her: "Full of grace, the Lord is with thee."

# XXVIII

## Invitation to Conversation

*I will utter my spirit to you, and show you my words (Prov. i. 23).*

Every form of culture leaves many traces of its influence upon the human race. We find evidence of this in the songs and poems which have been handed down from generation to generation; we see it again in the strange and beautiful monuments of architecture, domestic and civic, which persist through the changes of many centuries. In the matter of religion, which is the greatest factor in any culture, it is the same. Men must express themselves in outward forms; and in this manner they give themselves away, and other men will some day judge them by the evidence they have left behind.

If by some great tragedy men of the Western world were swept from the face of the earth, those who took their place would judge their predecessors' culture by those outward expressions which we have mentioned above. There would be many ugly things (for example, the instruments of war), not a little of our literature and art, by which they would think ill of us. But there would still remain for them to admire and wonder at the beauty of our religious monuments, the music, the art, and the great institutions of charity as a witness of the vast religious influence intermingled with less worthy aspects of our Western civilization.

Not least among the ruins which another people might find would be the evidence of devotion to one who was known by many titles, but who was most commonly described as the Virgin Mary, the Mother of God.

And if some curious professor from the East wished to know what the Christian faithful of the West thought and felt concerning the Virgin Mary, he could not do better than trace the love and devotion of the faithful by means of the many public and private forms of prayer which had been offered to her throughout the long centuries of Christian culture and civilization.

The reason for this is clear. It is in prayer, in the raising up of the mind and heart, that we most explicitly express ourselves. The pattern of our prayer is the pattern of our lives. Prayer reveals our most intimate thoughts, our fears, our love and our faith. Prayer is the human mode of expressing the aspirations and yearnings of the soul and spirit. However much we may cover up our sorrows and anxieties from our fellow-men, we are not afraid of revealing them to God, and to those friends of His and of ours who have found favor in His sight —the Virgin Mary and the Saints. Prayer also reveals the gratitude of men to God for the many ways and means that He has given them of seeking Him, and receiving help at His hands. Holy Scripture tells us that we cannot utter the name Jesus (in a meritorious way) unless we are inspired to do so by the Holy Spirit of God. Prayer, therefore, is also an indication of how, in what manner, we are influenced by the Divine Spirit of Love.

The Liturgy of the Catholic Church gives us the volume of prayer, the public expression of the Mystical Body of Christ; it is a revelation of the inner spirit of the members of Christ's Church in relation to God, the Virgin, and the Saints. Thus, the Liturgy reveals the inner life of the Church, letting us know something more of the influence of the Spirit of God upon the faithful.

It is in the liturgical prayers of the Church that we catch a further revelation of the Mother of God. It is by the prayers offered up by the faithful that we see what they expect of her; it is by their prayers of thanksgiving and gratitude that we find how much she has done for them.

In many instances we find the faithful using the words of the Mother of God herself to express their own sentiments. In other cases, we find the faithful using new titles in her honor, because under certain circumstances she has come to their aid. The whole chain of titles used in the Litany of Our Lady is an expression of Catholic tradition down the centuries, showing us the love and tender ties that exist between Mary and her children. To reflect upon these titles is to bring home to ourselves the reality of Mary's intervention in human affairs, her power to intercede for us, and the trust that we place in her prayers for us.

There is no doubt that the communion of will and mind, which is the essence of prayer, between ourselves and Mary has not only done honor to her to whom our prayers are addressed, but it has given each of us a new life in the Holy Spirit of God. The very fact of meditating upon the virtues and graces of the Mother of God, gives us cause to imitate them. The more we lift our minds to her, the more enlightened in the Spirit shall we be. The more our wills are united to her in prayer, the more readily shall we follow the inspirations given us during prayer by the Spirit of God. Thus, almost unconsciously will the Mother of God be molding us into a new and higher life—a life of spiritual peace and joy, of union with that Spirit whom she enshrined and who has given us into her charge, that by prayer, faith and imitation we may come to know, love and serve God, and conform ourselves to the Spirit by whom we are sealed unto the day of salvation.

# XXIX

## *Mystical Rose*

*Hear me, ye divine offspring, and bud forth as the rose (Ecclus., xxxix. 17).*

If we ask ourselves and try candidly to answer the question, what is the end and purpose of prayer and the Sacraments, we shall have to arrive at an answer which is normally disconcerting to the average Catholic: a supernatural sharing of life with God. To put it more clearly, the ultimate purpose of prayer and the Sacraments is a mystical union with God.

The reason why this answer is disconcerting, is because the average Catholic, while accepting the practice of his religious life with simplicity of faith, seldom analyzes the real meaning of the instruments of his religious life and habits. So closely wedded are his everyday acts of religion to those which he performs merely as a man among men, that he does not stop to think how tremendous is one act of prayer. Yet, we have the assurance of Holy Scripture that we cannot utter the name, Jesus, unless the Holy Spirit of God enables us to do so for His greater honor or our salvation. The average Catholic, taking so much for granted, does not stop to think of the chasm which lies between the world of nature to which he was originally born, and the supernatural world into which he has been adopted by grace. The man or woman who seldom falls into mortal sin, considers God as integral a part of his or her life as the people among whom he or she works, mingles, and passes the time of day.

This naturalness of the supernatural has it disadvantages as well as its obvious advantages. It is, in the first place, a very charming trait of those who have lived long in the atmosphere of the true faith; it has a disarming and reverent familiarity about it which is, in its turn, most disconcerting to those who are not of our faith. On the other hand, if the things of faith are taken too much for granted, they lose much of their power to accomplish the purpose for which they were intended. If the faculty of flying by his own power were given to man in order to reach a far and foreign land, it would frustrate the very purpose of the gift, if he exercised it merely in flying over his own country, never daring to fly out of sight of the familiar coast-line of his native shores. And the more familiar he became in the use of the faculty for his own enjoyment, the less likely would he consider the real purpose for which it was given him; namely, not to remain close to the things he knew, but to seek out the unknown and adventurous things across the seas.

Prayer and the Sacraments of grace, though built upon and incorporated in our human nature, were meant to carry us beyond the boundaries of nature, to transform us into the heights of God's love. If with St. Paul we were by grace "able to comprehend with all the saints what is the breadth and length and height and depth, and to know Christ's love which surpasses knowledge" (Eph., iii. 18-19), we must needs use with intelligence the gifts God has given us to do this thing to the fullest degree possible, not by our power, but by His.

Prayer and the Sacraments have as their ultimate aim the mystical union with God for all eternity. Ultimately we must come to that, if we are to be saved; indeed, that is our salvation. Every prayer lifts us by the wings of grace from this earth towards God. Every worthy reception of the Sacraments is the strengthening of the faculty to fly and be united with God. Yet, it is all too true that even the most sincere and zealous of Catholics fear to use these powers to go forward beyond a certain point, which we may call the margin of human experience. Any idea that they are called to a closer mystical union is as frightening to them as losing touch with their native earth. Perhaps, this is because they do not realize that the least conspicuous of God's graces is a mystical union of the creature with his Creator. Perhaps, it is owing to a familiarity with the supernatural which has made him forget the chasm between what we are by nature and what we have become by grace . Much more is this latent fear of the mystical due to a gravely wrong emphasis that has been made by biographical writers in the portrayal of the lives of the Saints.

It would be altogether misleading to suggest that the lives of the Saints in their union with God were ordinary, even in the supernatural order of things; no, many of their spiritual experiences were extraordinary to a marked degree. In many instances, nevertheless, the extraordinary sphere of their experiences has been overemphasized out of all proportion. The result of this overemphasis, over a long period, has been that the common run of Catholics have come to consider that there is a fundamental difference, in kind, between the means and ideals of ordinary Christian life (if we can ever call it that), and those which animated and gave purpose to the lives of the Saints. The ordinary Christian has come to regard any form of mystical union with God as entirely outside and beyond the possibility, or even the legitimate aspiration, of his own spiritual life.

A few minutes' quiet and balanced consideration of the mysteries of the indwelling of the Holy Spirit of God in the soul should immediately dispel any such harmful notion. A deeper appreciation of the spirituality of Mary, the Mystical Rose, should go far in assuring us that no such chasm exists between the adopted sons of God and His Saints. The gradual unfolding of the spiritual life and union of Mary with God should go far in dispelling that fear most of us have of surrendering ourselves to the divine influences of the Holy Spirit within us. Perhaps, one of the things which ties us to the mediocrity of our spirituality and union with God, is the notion that, if we give ourselves more fully to the consideration of the indwelling of the Spirit of God, we shall be less active in the ordinary duties of our state of life. We shall, if we are thus attentive to God, be less attentive to the things of earth which so encompass us. This is true, but in a way quite different from what we suppose. They will not be neglected, these duties of ours; they must not be neglected, for they are part of our vocation in life; but they will be accomplished in a new spirit, they will be given a new direction.

Did the Maid of Nazareth neglect the duties that were hers, because of her unsurpassed union with God? Were the Gifts of the Holy Spirit of God an impediment to the active charity of the Mother of Jesus among her neighbors? Was Mary less diligent in the duties of a wife and mother because she was "full of grace"?

The "considerations" which proceed from these few words on Mary, the Mystical Rose, cannot but convince us that we are all called to a certain mystical union with God. That the center and source of that union is in the indwelling of the Holy Spirit of God. How far that mystical union will lead us is hidden from our eyes. But this we do know, that it is part of our destiny to share in a mystical union with our God for all eternity. How far we shall go forward to that union now, is a matter for our own decision and generosity, and who knows how much depends on the present decision—perhaps the whole of our future!

It is in the unfolding of the Mystical Rose, that we shall find the greatest beauty of that life with God. In her life, revealed in the pages of the Gospels, we shall find no continued extraordinary phenomenon to affright us, no rigor to deter us, no denunciation to disquiet us. There lie the fragrance of her love, the lowliness of her station among men, the odor of her sanctity which has made her the Mystical Rose, the choice gift of God to men.

# XXX

# The Paradox

*He that made me, rested in my tabernacle (Ecclus., xxiv. 12).*

Tradition, the voice of the living Church, has given certain titles to the Virgin of Nazareth which are, to say the least, puzzling to those who have not been brought up in our faith. And, if we were ourselves asked for an explanation of them, we might be at a loss fully to explain them.

One such title of the Virgin Mary is that by which we call upon her as the Mother of our Creator. To one not fully imbued with the richness of faith and tradition this title is not only a paradox, but a contradiction. How can the creature be the Mother of her Creator? For the Catholic, to whom the Mystery of the Incarnation is the first principle of his faith, this paradox and contradiction is solved in the firm belief that the Word of God, "through whom the world was made" (John, i. 10), took flesh by the power of the Holy Ghost from the Virgin Mary, at the time of the Annunciation. The Catholic appreciates the deep and significant fact that the Son of Mary was a Divine Person, having, therefore, existence not only before He took flesh from her, but before all time. Nevertheless, the same faith teaches the Catholic that this Person became her Son with all the infinite attributes of His Divine Nature, nor could He in any sense be separated from them. "Who though he was by nature God, did not consider being equal to God a thing to be clung to, but emptied himself, taking the nature of a slave and being made like unto men. And appearing in the form of man, he humbled himself, becoming obedient to death, even to death on the cross" (Phil. ii. 6-8). Though His attributes—and among these, that of Creator—remain forever His, yet He finds a way, through Mary the Virgin, to put aside the power of His glory—that "glory," He tells us, "which I had with thee before the world existed" (John, xvii. 5)—by taking human nature, and yet retaining all that was divine.

The Liturgy has a beautiful phrase by which the

Church expresses this mystery on the Feast of the Nativity, giving praise to the Virgin Mary: "Because Him whom the heavens could not contain within their limits, thou hast borne in thy womb."

The glory which has come to the Virgin of Nazareth is through the unique association of hers with the Person of the Word of God. The fact of the Incarnation could bring about no change in the Person or Nature of God (that is obvious from His very Being), but it could and did bring about a unique relationship in the Motherhood of Mary.

We have seen how the Holy Spirit of God brought about the conception of St. John the Baptist, both concerning his miraculous coming into existence and his sanctification in his mother's womb. But the parallel with the mysterious birth of Christ ceases at that point. The motherhood of Elizabeth, though miraculous, was a natural relationship of mother and son. The Motherhood of Mary, through the overshadowing of the Holy Ghost, was wholly divine in its origin, and it was divine in its relationship as between mother and Son. The Cause of His conception was wholly outside the realm of human agency, apart from her coöperation.

We may also note that, whereas St. Luke gives us the human story of the coming of the Son of God in the opening pages of the Holy Gospels, St. John, on the contrary, opens his account of the life of Christ with the challenging narrative of the "life" which He possessed from all eternity: "In the beginning was the Word, and the Word was with God; and the Word was God. He was in the beginning with God. All things were made through him, and without him was made nothing that has been made" (John, i. 1-3).

How impossible it is, then, for us to dissociate the Virgin Mary from the fact of our faith, that she was in very deed the Mother of our Creator— the instrument of bringing us into personal contact with the Word made Flesh!

But is she not the Mother of our Creator in quite another sense? When we sing *Veni Creator Spiritus,* can we put aside the thought that the coming of the Holy Spirit, our re-creation in grace, is fundamentally bound up in the mystery by which Mary became the Mother of God? Certainly, the whole of Catholic spirituality and the expression of the Mystical Body of Christ in the Liturgy bids us pay tribute to Mary, as the Mother of our re-creation in Christ her Divine Son.

We can truly say that Mary's *fiat*, "Be it done to me according to thy word" (Luke, i. 38), was as potent in the supernatural sphere, as was God's "Fiat lux" (Let there be light) in the natural. In both of these overshadowings of the Holy Spirit of God something entirely new took place; all the wealth of our natural world came into being in the one instance; in the other, all the tremendous gifts of our supernatural life found the Source of their being. At this second *fiat*, the Holy Spirit of God made Mary the instrument of His creative power, all depended upon her word, and at her word our eternal life with God became possible, through the mystery of our incorporation with Him.

The fact that Mary had contained within herself the Creator of all things, truly raises her above all other creatures, but not beyond them. Instead, the very purpose for which she was made instrumental in our new life with God, was that He might reach out to us in a new and closer union with us. Mary, then, as the Mother of our Creator, takes on the new prerogative of "Mother of all the living, the Second Eve."

We have recalled so often that the Holy Spirit chose Mary as His own special instrument in "renewing the face of the earth," that earth of which we are formed, and which must be reformed in Christ. Perhaps the consideration of the Virgin, as Mother of our Creator, will bring home to us how fundamental is this change in our lives by grace. It is not as if God in redeeming us were merely covering up the faults and failings of our human nature; it is much more true to fact to speak of His changing that nature, lifting it from the human to the supernatural plane of life.

This re-creation took place in that historic moment when the Holy Spirit overshadowed the Immaculate Virgin, when a new world of grace, of peace, of love, trembled on the lips of Mary; at her *fiat,* there was a new light, the Light of the World.

173

# XXXI

# The Savior's Mother

*And behold, thou shalt conceive in thy womb, and shalt bring forth a son, and shalt call his name Jesus (Luke, i. 31).*

When we considered the Feast of the Nativity in the Third Joyful Mystery, we emphasized the fact that the world of men as a whole are little conscious of the need of salvation. This does not for a minute mean that they are not conscious that much is wrong with the world. Indeed, every form of public life is marked by the knowledge of a breakdown in human relationships and happiness. Nevertheless, human individuals are little aware of the flaw that exists in human nature itself. We are all, and more especially those living without faith, apt to think and to act upon the assumption that all would be well if our neighbors, or the circumstances of our life, were changed. We never seem to consider that the real change, and the only one which will bring permanent settlement, is essentially a change from within ourselves.

This lack of realization of a fundamental need of salvation from a wrong that is deep in human nature, is quite a modern trend. It is sufficient to note here that it has its basis in what is known as humanitarianism, which is a long word meaning our own self-sufficiency. This sense of self-satisfaction is derived from the wondrous progress that has been made in the last hundred years in every department of human life—in every department except one, the spiritual, the art of living together.

If there was one thought uppermost in the hearts and desires of the people from whom Mary of Nazareth derived her conception of life, it was this consciousness of the need of salvation, and of a Savior. There are those, of course, who would belittle this fact by assuring us that this was merely because the Jewish people were at the time, and had been on many occasions, in a state of semi-servitude. But any one sufficiently acquainted with the history of the Jewish people will realize that this sense of a need of salvation was as predominant in the days of their triumph as it was in their times of exile and humiliation.

The concept of a Savior was born in the dim ages of man's history. It first found expression in the words of the Book of Genesis. It is significant for us that it was expressed in connection with a woman. To the enemy of mankind God said: "I will put enmities between thee and the Woman, and thy seed and her seed; she shall crush thy head, and thou shalt lie in wait for her heel" (Gen., iii. 15). The whole history of the Chosen People is the history of a people in travail for the coming of a Savior.

When the Holy Spirit was to overshadow the Virgin of Nazareth, the messenger of God left no possible doubt in her mind as to the historic position she was to have; as to the fact that, at long last, the fullness of God's promise was to become a reality, and that she, the Maid, was to be the Mother of the Messiah. "And behold, thou shalt conceive in thy womb, and shalt bring forth a son, and thou shalt call his name Jesus. He shall be great, and shall be called the son of the Most High; and the Lord God will give him the throne of David his father, and he shall be king over the house of Jacob forever; and of his kingdom there shall be no end" (Luke, i. 31-33). To one versed, as Mary was, in the traditions and writings of her people this message could mean only one thing, so clearly did it fulfill the word spoken by Isaias: "Behold, a virgin shall conceive and bear a son: and his name shall be called Emmanuel" (Isa., vii. 14). And this was to be a sign given by God Himself of the coming of the Savior.

Christian tradition, and indeed the explicit teaching of the Church, has always connected the "Woman" in Genesis with Mary the Virgin of Nazareth. Christian tradition has always associated Mary with the crushing of the power of evil. That this power of evil surrounds us, few would be willing to deny. We are also conscious that there is something within human nature itself which man has to resist and overcome. It is here that the idea and concept of salvation is most pregnant with meaning for us.

As long as men neglect the fundamental fact that each of us is in need of personal salvation, so long will their efforts at social security be in vain. However humbling the recognition may be that we ourselves are lacking in the power to remedy our weakness, until this first approach is made, no amount of coöperation among men of good will will suffice to heal the weakness that is in all. And is it humbling to think that it is the Son of God Himself who is to become our Healer? "The Spirit of the Lord is upon me; because he has anointed me; to bring good news to the poor he has sent me, to proclaim to the captives release, and sight to the blind; to set at liberty the oppressed, to proclaim the acceptable year of the Lord, and the day of recompense" (Luke, iv. 18, 19).

These last words of Isaias, quoted by St. Luke, were familiar to the Maid of Nazareth as she knelt to accept the honor of being the Mother of the Savior of the world. We have pondered in these pages upon the intervention of the Mother of God on behalf of those whom she has by right called her children. As Mother of the Savior, she is fully conscious of the deep wound which human nature suffered as a result of original sin, from which she was preserved in her Immaculate Conception by reason of her office as Mother of our Savior.

Mary, the Mother of our Savior, is well aware that our strength against the powers of evil is not in the material progress that men have made; it is not in the gathering of men together in conferences, however well-meant they may be; our reliance must be in the strength that comes from holiness—from the power of the Holy Spirit of God, whom she enshrined.

Mary, more than any other, is aware that salvation does not consist in some magical transformation of man by which he becomes some new being wholly different from his fellows. The Mother of Good Counsel knows that salvation starts rather in a fundamental new being, and from *that point* is a gradual growth in the Holy Spirit of God. It is rather by the transformation of man's attitude towards his own capability (as being sufficient to combat evil) to a humble regard of his own powers and a consciousness that his strength is in God. Were they not prophetic words of hers in her *Magnificat?* "And for generation upon generation is his mercy, to those who fear him. He has shown might with his arm, he has scattered the proud in the conceit of their heart. He has put down the mighty from their thrones, and has exalted the lowly. He has filled the hungry with good things, and the rich he has sent away empty" (Luke, i. 50-53).

# XXXII

# *Knights in Armor*

*All these are gathered together, they are come to thee: thy sons shall come from afar (Isa., lx. 4).*

The sons and daughters of Mary, the Mother of God, are innumerable, their names would form a formidable litany of their own.

When we refer to Mary, Queen of Confessors, we do so in a twofold sense. We acclaim her as Queen of all those men who have gained and will in the future receive the eternal reward of faithfulness to her Divine Son's discipleship, whether this is manifest to men at large, or their grace and holiness are hidden from our eyes. In a more particular way, we know her as the Queen of Confessors, because she has been the inspiration of those great historic characters who have been witnesses of Christ in every century: Saints, Fathers of the Church, Doctors and more recent apostles of Christ.

Here, again, there is need for selection from the

multitude of Saints who have won the crown of glory by confessing Christ, and have made Mary their special advocate and model. To illustrate the profound influence that the Mother of God has had upon the Confessors of Christ, we choose those who have added most, in recurring centuries, to the honor and glory of the Virgin of Nazareth.

In the context of these pages, the first great name which springs to our minds, when considering the sons of Mary, is the name of Ephraem—"The Harp of the Holy Spirit," as he came to be called.

The poetry of the deacon, St. Ephraem, became famous in the fourth century in the Eastern Church. He was eloquent in defense of the Faith of Christ, and his poetry showed a penetrating love of the Mother of God. To-day, we read his verses on the Feast Days of the Virgin, and we are no longer left in wonderment at the love and devotion which the Mother of God has always claimed in the Eastern Church. Here was an Apostle of the Divine Maternity, at the moment when civilization, our civilization, was first holding the alliance of all man, was first rising from the pagan Empire of Rome and Greece. This apostle and poet of the

Holy Ghost left to the world a monumental work of praise to the Mother of God, to her honor and our greater richness in understanding.

Three centuries later the Holy Spirit of God gave to the Church another great defender of the prerogatives of Mary—in particular, concerning the doctrine of the Assumption of the Mother of God into Heaven, and our honoring her in different forms of art. St. John Damascene, the last of the Greek Fathers, has enriched the Church with his writings on those mysteries which so directly concern the Motherhood of Mary, and given us an insight into the tradition, the living voice of the teaching Church, at a time which forms a link between the teaching of the Eastern and Western Fathers of the Church. At a critical time in the formation of the external life of the Church, owing to widespread heresy, the Holy Spirit of God, ever present in the Mystical Body, did not fail to raise up a defender of the Mother of God, and one to whom future teachers might turn in similar circumstances, in manifesting the continuity of teaching concerning the prerogatives of Mary as Mother and Virgin.

How closely Mary allies herself with the life and
work of the Holy Ghost in the Church is clearly
illustrated in her influence upon the spiritual greatness of St. Bernard. We may say that a whole
spiritual order of men have been formed and
moulded by the Mother of God through her great
champion: and this at a time when the fervor of
the faithful had fallen to a dangerously low level.
St. Bernard in his largeness of heart, in his deep
charity for men, did not only add to the context
of ascetical and mystical theology through his com-
mentaries on Holy Scripture, but he, almost for the
first time, made Mary the vehicle of the whole of
a man's ascent to God. He truly looked upon her
as the "Mother of the Living," the New Eve, in
and through whom we were best able to come to
her Divine Son. This great reformer, under her
Good Counsel, not only added yet another religious
family to the Church, but through his writings
and preaching, through his apostolic missions, he
reawakened the whole of Christendom to a greater
love and fidelity to Christ. In all these labors Mary
was his inspiration, her name was always in his
heart and upon his lips. The traditional love of the

Mother, which has always been the hall-mark of the sons of St. Bernard, is no less effective to-day than it was in the past—witness the Trappists. In this country, owing not a little to these men, that particular form of devotion to Mary which is considered under her title of Mystical Rose has burst into new life, and Mary has called to herself many of those who, in these distressing days, seek that peace and union with God which comes so readily to the men who wear her mantle of purity in the silence of the cloister.

Little need be said in detail of the great numbers of Confessors whom Mary inspired in that period of faith known as the Middle Ages. All that we have said, and much more, concerning the holy Mysteries of the Rosary owes its origin to this special gift of hers to her beloved son, St. Dominic. The patronage which the Mother of God gave to the founder of the Order of Preachers has been fully returned by the great devotion its members have shown to the Holy Virgin. Among many others of the Order, the two great Doctors of the Church, St. Albert the Great and the Angelic Doctor, stand out as writers and poets of her prerogatives and virtues.

That other great bulwark of the Church in these times, the members of the Order of St. Francis were no less zealous in their love and honor to the Queen of Confessors. It was from the hands of Mary, at her Shrine of Our Lady of the Angels, that the Little Poor Man, Francis of Assisi, obtained the then unique privilege, the Great Pardon. It is this same Order which, through its love of Mary, has given to the Christian world the pious practice of the *Angelus*. It was a son of St. Francis who gave us the *Stabat Mater*. St. Anthony was the special Apostle of the Mother of God.

The names of St. Ignatius, St. Francis Xavier and Saint Grignon de Montfort show how this traditional love of Mary, Queen of Confessors, has been kept alive and enlarged by men forming a link between our own days and those of the centuries past.

It will be noted that each of those whom we have picked at random, and those many other names which must have been recalled by the reader, were men of truly apostolic zeal. Each in his own way enriched the Mystical Body of Christ by his work and labors. In his own life, and among those to whom he gave his life, there was a new and refreshing "mission" of the Holy Spirit of Love.

Mary, the Queen of Confessors, is thus chosen by God to work through men, to draw them to herself, that she may impart to them that Spirit of Love whom she enshrined. Then it is, when they have learned from the Seat of Wisdom and the Mother of Good Counsel, that she sends them forth that the earth may be recreated and renewed, and all may come to the harbor of salvation, led thither by the "Morning Star."

# XXXIII

## Creative Love

*I will understand in the unspotted way, when thou shalt come to me" (Ps., c. 2).*

No doubt, there are a thousand and one explanations for the lack of devotion to the Holy Spirit of God. And if we are wise, we shall not too readily accept any one as a full explanation in itself. We must remember that the practices of devotion belong to the living Church. It is noticeable that certain trends of devotion—for instance, to the Sacred Humanity of Christ, to the Abiding Presence of Christ in the Holy Eucharist—only became "common practice" after centuries of development. And very possibly it will take more centuries of devotion and practice in these—if we may use with reverence the term—more concrete forms of devotion, before people as a whole pay more outward honor to the Holy Spirit of God.

However, when we pass from the general practice of the faithful to individual devotion, it is easier and safer to ascertain and state the obstacles to a cult of the Holy Spirit. Every theologian and —what is more to the point—every confessor will agree that neglect of devotion to the Holy Ghost is both a cause *and* result of a lack of purity. Impurity of mind or body is incompatible with true devotion to the Holy Spirit of Love. The converse is equally true; where there is Christian purity, it is there that we shall find devotion to the Spirit of God.

This will be fairly clear to any instructed Catholic. What may escape the attention even of such a one, is the tragedy of this divorce between the basis of purity and the Spirit of Love. The Operation of the Holy Spirit is made known to us by faith and by the fruits of the Spirit within the soul. What is the connection between this indwelling of the Spirit of Love and the virtue of purity?

Purity, chastity, is too often considered in a negative manner—in its perversion and frustration. Really, it is a virtue which not merely guards and protects the power of the creative human love; it is not merely a guard set over something rebellious, something which is condemned to imprisonment. It is this attitude towards purity which often makes its practice most difficult, which sometimes leads to the very rebellion we try to avoid.

The power of creative love in the first instance belongs to God alone. We ourselves are what we are because that love has found external expression. All the wonders of the supernatural and the natural order of things are part of that immense and infinite power. The power of human love belongs, therefore, to God; man's active part in its expression is necessarily joined to and bound up in that creative power of God's love.

The virtue of purity is positively given us, as intelligent and loving agents of God, to coördinate the power of creative love with the creative Love of God: that these may be one, even as the expression of love makes man and woman two in one flesh.

Human love finds one means of expression through the sexual passions; it is the *intentional* use of these passions which makes them good or bad, in the moral sense. The virtue of purity, or the vice of impurity, is the positive cause by which these powers are used either in conformity with or contrary to the creative love of God.

The primary purpose, then, of the virtue of purity is *not* guardianship of our passions—though it has that also as its object—but the intelligent and willing union of the expression of human love with divine love, making the former holy and fruitful. The virtue of purity enables us to observe the laws which God has made concerning the expression of *our* love, or non-expression of it, according to the circumstances He has laid down. There can be no union of human love with His without this. The secondary purpose of the virtue of purity, owing to original sin, is to ensure that the sexual passions do not gain command over the mind and will. But if there had been no injury to man through original sin, purity would still have had a predominant place in man's power of creative love.

Self-indulgence in the sexual passions, or an indulgence in which the creative power of God is positively excluded, has special reference to our relationship with the Holy Ghost, because both of these are an exclusion on our part of God's love.

The bare summary we have given of the close

relationship between purity and the indwelling of the Holy Spirit of God is sufficient to suggest why Mary has always been the model and example of all Christians in the matter of purity.

The very uniqueness of the fruitfulness of Mary's virginity emphasizes the power of God, but, as the hymn of thanksgiving expresses it, God did not disdain the Virgin's womb. So sublime was the purity of this Virgin, in body and in soul, that the very Son of God took flesh from her flesh, and gave to her not only the crown of the Virgin, but the honor and prerogative of maternity.

For those who are yet single, but who anticipate that they will be called to the vocation of Christian marriage, and may thereby fulfill in their own human love the designs of God, there can be no better or more secure preparation than devotion through Mary to the Holy Spirit. The sweet discipline that is required of those who wish to cultivate a love of the Holy Ghost, will give them that peace and strength necessary for a vocation so intimately bound up with the creative power of Divine Love.

To those already bound by the vows of marriage the Holy Spirit will, through Mary's intercession, give that fortitude, self-sacrifice, and enduring faithfulness required of their station in life.

To those who have bound themselves more closely to God by the vow of chastity, the Holy Spirit Himself will be the reward of their purity of soul and body; their souls will be His shrines, their bodies His living temples.

All the Gifts of the Holy Spirit, if truly valued and used by us, have their own particular fruits. He is ever creative in His love; where He makes His abiding presence, there will be found the fruits of His power.

If in the world to-day we find so little of this Christian purity, it is because of the neglect of this essential devotion to Him. "By their fruits shall ye know them" (Matt., vii. 16). Where passion is separated from love, where it rules apart from the Love of the Spirit, there will be no peace, but only conflict and frustration; no creation of life, but the desecration of the Temple of God.

# XXXIV

# The Word Made Flesh

*Come, eat my Bread, and drink the Wine which I have mingled for you (Prov., ix. 5).*

"The Word was made flesh and dwelt amongst us" (John, i. 14). We have considered from many aspects this mystery of divine love, in which the Holy Spirit overshadowed the Virgin of Nazareth to give Life to the world. There remains one further aspect of the Word made Flesh, which is of personal importance to each and every one of us.

It is profoundly true to say that the whole spiritual preparation which the Holy Spirit of God made in regard to the Blessed Virgin, had one immediate end and purpose—that she might be the Tabernacle of the Most High: "Thou shalt conceive in thy womb, and shalt bring forth a son, and thou shalt call his name Jesus. He shall be great, and shall be called the Son of the Most High . . . the power of the Most High shall overshadow thee;

and therefore the Holy One to be born shall be called the Son of God" (Luke, i. 31-32, 35).

Close to her heart Mary possessed the Son of the Living God. Mary had no power to bring God into her bosom; He was there by the operation of the Holy Spirit of God—really, truly present for nine months. During that time Mary gave back to her God something of herself, something so intimate that it required the creative Spirit of God to make this gift to the Second Person of the Holy Trinity; she gave to the Son of God, by the overshadowing of the Spirit, her own very flesh and blood. Can we wonder now at the perfection of that preparation of grace and purity with which the Holy Ghost made ready within her the shrine of the indwelling of God made man!

Yes, Mary, by the power of the Holy Ghost, clothed the Son of God with her flesh, gave to Him the human form of man—gave to Him the living blood of man, which was to be poured out for our salvation. St. Augustine expresses this profound mystery in four simple words: "Caro Christi, Caro Mariæ" (Flesh of Christ, Flesh of Mary).

In our approach to the Sacrament of Love, it

must make us deeply humble to think that we enshrine the same Son of the Most High in a tabernacle so little prepared for this divine communion with our God. Yet, there is no effective means of preparation, coming from our own resources, upon which we can rely. We may well ask the Virgin of Nazareth: "How can this be done?" And there is but one answer to that question: "The Holy Spirit will come upon thee, and the power of the Most High will overshadow thee."

If Christ is to be formed within us, it is impossible that this can come about except through the power of God Himself. This communion with God is made through the medium of the humanity of Christ—the reception of His Sacred Body and Blood. But it is not a mere corporal union that Christ has in mind: "Not as your fathers ate the manna, and died. He who eats this bread shall live forever" (John, vi. 59). It is a union with the Living Spirit of God.

It will be seen that the invocation of the Spirit of Love is not so much a result of our union with Christ, much less should our devotion to Him be something accidental or fitful; the Holy Spirit is the Divine Cause of our union with Christ. We lend our body, our flesh and blood as the instrument, as a vehicle of our union with the Body and Blood of Christ, with His humanity; but it is the power, the overshadowing, of the Holy Spirit of Love which makes this physical union fruitful in the spirit; and this is the real reason for which this Mystery of Love was instituted.

Mary was the vehicle of the Mystery of the Incarnation; we are the vehicles of fruitfully bearing the Incarnate Word of God, by the preparation and the "act" of grace of the Spirit of Love, whereby we are not merely corporally bearing Christ in our hearts, but are effectively one with Him, Body, Soul and Divinity.

Just as the Holy Spirit of God, through the Virgin Mary, gave to the world the Source and Center of all salvation, "through him to win back all things, whether on earth or in heaven, into union with himself, making peace with them through his blood, shed on the Cross," so too it is by the Holy Ghost that salvation is made personally ours. . . . "Unless a man be born again of water and the

Spirit he cannot enter into the Kingdom of God" (John, iii. 5).

By the overshadowing of the Holy Spirit, Christ even now in His humanity and Divinity, becomes the Source and Center of our *personal* salvation. The Flesh and Blood of Christ were the instruments of our salvation on the Cross by which we were *all* saved; the Flesh and Blood of Christ within us are the instruments of our own *personal* salvation. For this reason the Holy Spirit of God has sanctified us through the Sacraments of the Church, just as He abundantly prepared Mary to be the Tabernacle of the Most High. Each of the Sacraments from Baptism to Extreme Unction has a special significance in its relationship to the Center and Source of our spiritual life, the Body and Blood of Christ. Each in its own particular way prepares, restores, and strengthens that Living Source of grace—the Sacrament, the Presence of Christ in the soul, coming to us in His Flesh and Blood, Soul and Divinity.

Once long ago, the Word was made Flesh for all mankind; daily, the Word is made Flesh in His Sacramental Presence for the individuals who have been overshadowed by the Spirit of Love. This startling reality of the work of the Holy Ghost in our union of love with the Incarnate Word is no less actual than that miraculous indwelling of the Word within the womb of the Virgin Mother. Mary the Virgin received through the Holy Spirit a new relationship, that of Motherhood and Spouse; we, through the same Spirit, receive the relationship of sons of God and brethren in Christ. When we think that it was Mary who gave of her flesh and blood that the Incarnate Word might be given to us in the Sacrament of Love, we more readily appreciate that the term "Mother" has a new significance as regards ourselves: "Caro Christi, Caro Mariæ" (Flesh of Christ, Flesh of Mary)!

In a manner quite unique, Mary could say of the Infant whom she nursed in Bethlehem: "This is my Child, my Flesh and Blood—and yet His, who created all things out of nothing!" When that same Body was taken down from the Cross, after it had been delivered into the hands of wicked men for us, when bloodless it lay in her lap on Calvary, how closely Mary was identified with our Ransom!

As we receive the Precious Body and Blood of Mary's Son, can we not the more readily call upon her that she would make known to us the power of the Spirit of Love, that our reception may be effective and vital, that the Son of God may take form and character within us, that we may be identified with Him, that we may feel the movement of Divine life within us, that we may give to Him the fullness of our humanity, the fullness of our love?

# XXXV

## *Compassion*

*Your mercy is as a morning cloud, and as the dew that goeth away in the morning (Osee, vi. 4).*

There are very many ways in which the soul of Mary has "magnified" the Lord. As we have suggested elsewhere, Mary is the Mirror of God, who is Justice in the widest sense of that term. Among the many attributes of God which the Virgin of Nazareth has reflected for us, none has had greater appeal, few have done more for mankind, than that of mercy. For this reason Mary has become known to men as the Mother of Mercy.

It is a strange paradox of the religious life that those who are nearest to the common run of sinners find it hardest of all to forgive; that those who are most removed from sin find it always in their heart to show mercy and compassion. There are, among others, two explanations for this strange behavior, though these two are really one.

Firstly, all sin is selfishness. It is an indulgence in our own wilfulness, in opposition to the will of our Creator. Even though we are free from the more serious forms of sin, we are still tied by a hundred and one habits of wilfulness, of sinfulness, of a lack of generosity in surrendering our will to God.

Now, mercy is the expression of compassion (suffering with). Constant indulgence in our own wilfulness dries up, little by little, the well of sympathy within us. If we do not easily feel sorrow for our own state of sinfulness, how can we hope to feel sorrow for the sinfulness of others? (Heaven forbid that we should confuse that wishy-washy sentiment that some sinners have for others, a form of self-pity for those like ourselves, with the real stuff from which compassion comes!) Where the sources of sorrow are dry and arid, there cannot be any form of compassion: mercy is impossible.

Those who are freed to a greater or lesser degree from sin, are still more conscious of their aptitude towards sin; though their wills are not attached to sin, they are conscious of the tendency towards evil; they are, because they are free, also conscious of the bondage and slavery of sin. They can and do feel real compassion for sinners, because, being no longer bound by selfishness, their hearts and love go out towards others. They have lost, to a greater or lesser degree, the element of self-centeredness that is in most of us.

The second explanation of this paradox is this: sinners seldom show mercy to their fellows for the obvious reason that they are so far removed from the likeness of Christ, for his Spirit is not in them. Do you remember Christ's first sermon to the townsfolk of Nazareth? It began with the words of Isaias: "The Spirit of the Lord is upon me, because he has anointed me, to bring good news to the poor he has sent me, to proclaim to the captives release, and sight to the blind; to set at liberty the oppressed, to proclaim the acceptable year of the Lord, and the day of recompense" (Luke, iv. 18, 19).

"The Spirit of the Lord is upon me"—the Spirit of Love, of Compassion, the Spirit who was to cry through parched and battered lips: "Father, forgive them for they do not know what they are doing" (Luke, xxiii. 34). Once He was to tell the religious rulers of the people: "But go, and learn what this means: 'I desire mercy, and not sacrifice.' For I have come to call sinners, not the just" (Matt, ix. 13).

If these words, at the beginning of Christ's ministry, caused surprise to His neighbors in Nazareth, so that they "marvelled at the words of grace that came from his mouth" (Luke, iv. 22), they gave only joy to the heart of His Mother as she heard them. Mary knew that words were to pass into deeds, that the prophecy her Son used as a text was to be fulfilled in a manner none could then guess: that, with the coming of the New Testament, "mercy and truth have met each other; justice and peace have kissed" (Ps., lxxxiv. 11).

If compassion is the foundation of mercy, Mary fully entered into that sorrow-sharing on Calvary, both with the Divine Victim who offered Himself on the Cross for our Redemption, and for all of those for whom He paid the price in His Blood.

It is the tradition of the faithful that, at the moment when Christ passed from this world to the Father, He placed all the treasury of the Redemption in the hands of His Mother, that she might bestow all that He had won for us, according to her merciful love for us.

If it is freedom from sin, from selfishness, that alone leaves room for mercy, how full of compassion must the Immaculate Heart of Mary be for those who have been redeemed in the Blood of her Son!

"God's Mother was herself the recipient of God's mercy. She knew what mercy meant. When she chanted her *Magnificat*, she spoke of 'His mercy from generation to generation.' She realized that it was God's mercy that dealt with her. God's mercy made her a Mother, His Mother. God's mercy led her through all her ways." * God's mercy, we may add, gave to her the first great, and indeed unique, outpouring of the Holy Spirit of Love. We must remember that one of the great fruits of the indwelling of the Holy Ghost is abounding charity towards others. The holiness with which the Holy Spirit endows us does not in any sense leave us in isolation from others; it is, on the contrary, a consuming love, all-embracing.

---

* Words of Fr. Bede Jarrett, O.P., Sermon on Our Lady of Lourdes.

The mercy of the Mother of God has found its expression in many ways. We shall never know until the Day of Judgment the multitude of sinners who have found the grace of forgiveness at her hands. Her great sorrows have been the means of winning the hardest of sinners to repentance. This Mother of Compassion has sent her sons and daughters into the four corners of the world to win souls to her Divine Son, into the highways and byways of the world to compel them to come in. In every sanctuary of her Son there is the figure of Mary, hands outstretched in mercy and compassion. Her mercy is active in the work of redemption among those baptized in Christ, but who have fallen by the wayside; it is no less active among those who know not the Face of Christ and His Saving Name—men and women hidden beneath superstition and the darkness of paganism.

The spouse of Mary, the Holy Spirit, has given this special prerogative of mercy to her, for His very purpose of overshadowing her was to give love to the world which knew it not. Justice is of the Father, Redemption of the Son, Merciful Love of the Holy Ghost.

# XXXVI

## *Picking and Choosing*

*Let us choose to us judgment, and let us see among ourselves what is the best (Job, xxxiv. 4).*

The definition of a virtue does not always convey to us its *fullest* meaning. A definition gives us the meaning of a thing in itself, the ideal. There is an 'accepted meaning,' which shows us that same thing, not as it is in itself, but as we find it actually in practice. Take, for instance, the virtue of prudence. We may define it as a virtue by which we constantly choose the best means towards the attainment of a given purpose in life. Obviously this is a good and desirable virtue to possess as thus defined in the abstract. Yet, to many, there is a ring about the word "prudence" which we do not like. Prudence to the modern ear has something about it which we associate with "stuffiness," with a lack of generosity, of openness of character.

Here, we are meeting again that same problem

of the corruption of the meanings of words, as we did when we considered the subject of piety. Like this latter term, the meaning of prudence, in moral and spiritual theology, has nothing about it from which we should shrink. On the contrary, it is a virtue which we should highly prize.

Human prudence has perhaps fallen into disrepute because it has so often been associated and motivated by selfishness. When we think of this virtue, we often have in mind the careful business man, the man who has come out on top because he has always played safe, he has seldom taken a chance. Here, more often than not, the chief guide has been self-interest, and however self-centered we may be ourselves, we always despise this failing in others. The heroes and heroines of to-day, as in the past, are not noted for their prudence in this latter sense; they are those who have gone forward without regard to themselves, those who have taken very big chances in life. It would almost be more true to say of them that they were rash, rather than prudent.

Perhaps we may come back to a true meaning of prudence by considering one or two points in the lives of those who have combined, in a remarkable degree, the halo of sanctity and the luster of heroism. St. Francis of Assisi, who did away with his own hope of inheritance and gave all things to the poor, was considered both rash and imprudent by the youth of Assisi, among whom he figured as a leader. The subsequent history of Francis shows that he was always daring in the things he did—as when to convert the Saracens he walked into their camp without means of protection—and yet we find that both the giving away of his worldly goods and the risking of his life were, in fact, but means which he chose to attain an end. This is the true definition of prudence. He chose to give all that he possessed because, after due thought and enlightenment, he found that this was *the* way, the heroic way, to possess the fullness of Christ. He was willing to risk the very poor opinion he had of the worth of his own life, to rescue those souls which he thought to be above price in the eyes of God.

When Damien stepped ashore on the Island of Molokai, he unknowingly stepped into the limelight that belongs only to heroes; but those in the boat which set him ashore thought him the most rash and imprudent of young men. Here again a man had weighed in the balance the values of earthly loves and friendships against the friendship of God, and had found the former wanting; he remembered the words: "Greater love than this no one has, that one lay down his life for his friends" (John, xv. 13). He was no less prudent than he was heroic.

Prudence then can certainly wear the garb of heroism. From the standpoint of human affairs, it can take on the appearance of rashness, almost of foolishness. It is the scale of values that gives this misleading twist to the expression of prudence.

In itself, prudence is the right choice of means to an end, to a purpose in life. It gives a right direction to the power of action. It is prudence, in the long view, which governs the saying of Christ: "For what does it profit a man, if he gain the whole world, but suffer the loss of his own soul? Or what will a man give in exchange for his soul?" (Matt., xvi. 26). In the realm of the spiritual life, it is often true that desperate means have to be taken to gain our end. This is because the prize is so great— eternal knowledge, love, and union with God. From a human viewpoint these means will often

seem lacking in prudence, in carefulness for ourselves. This is, because, alas, the human way of
thinking cannot see things in the light of grace; we
cannot see the end towards which divine prudence
under the influence of the Holy Spirit is leading us.
Only when the Saints of God have achieved their
purpose, do men see the heroism and wisdom of
their actions, and they are forced to exclaim with
St. Paul: "O the depth of the riches of the wisdom
and of the knowledge of God! How incompre-
hensible are his judgments, and how unsearchable
his ways!" (Rom., xi. 33).

That this fundamental moral virtue of prudence
governed the life of the Mother of God, there can
be no doubt. However, when we come to illustrate
the fact, the task is not so easy. The reason for this
difficulty is not far to seek: her life was largely hidden in God.

We have seen how the Gifts of the Holy Spirit,
of Counsel, Understanding, Knowledge, were fully
developed in the spiritual life of Mary. The very
exercise and effects of these Gifts are themselves an
illustration of the place that the moral virtue of

prudence had in her life. These Gifts are the hand-maids of the moral virtues, given to us in Baptism, but infused into the soul of the Mother of God at the moment of her Immaculate Conception. They in her, as they do in us, disposed her mind and heart to exercise the more fundamental virtue of pru-dence in all her actions, choosing in each instance of action that which most fully made her truly the Handmaid of the Lord.

A clear instance of her divine prudence, as op-posed to human prudence, which sees only our own welfare and interests, is shown in her journey to Bethlehem in the days of her expectation. Human prudence was all against such a journey at that time. Divine enlightenment caused her to set aside her own concern, and, in doing just that, she ful-filled the Divine Will of God, that her Son should be born in Bethlehem of Judea.

Mary Most Prudent, if we only make her our ally, will teach us this divine art of following in all things the inspirations of the Holy Ghost, through the impulse of His Gifts. It is not always an easy art to acquire, but it is one that is essential if we are to reach that perfection for which we were born, and for which God has given us so rich a fund of means; and the ultimate prudence of which is manifested in the lives of the Saints.

# XXXVII

## *Among Men*

*For her sake I shall have glory among the multitude (Wis., viii. 10).*

We have suggested that it is a matter of experience that sanctity is always accompanied by a solid devotion to the Mother of God. We must not think of this as a kind of necessity, or obligation of faith, without which we cannot be saved. But it is something implicit in the very nature of holiness, that our faith should also find expression in devotion to one who was so close to God. Devotion, as distinct from believing, is an expression of the will; love enters into devotion, which therefore is a free offering of our willing service to the Mother of God.

So universal, both in time and place, is devotion to the Virgin that we must attribute it to the influence of the Holy Spirit, who, we have seen, alone guides the spiritual life of the Church and each of its members. We can see the reason for this, because the reign of Mary over the hearts of men has had, and was meant to have, a very definite effect upon the organization and the work of the Church throughout the centuries.

To-day no one can deny the presence of Mary, the Comforter of the Afflicted, at Lourdes. What a vast influence, within our own short memories, has not Our Lady of Fatima had upon the lives of thousands of men and women throughout the war-stricken world! Who would be able to count the souls who have returned to the exercise of their faith, of penance and sorrow, at the invitation of Our Lady of Fatima in the countless novenas which have been offered in her honor?

In what are known as the Ages of Faith, the presence of Our Lady was felt throughout the whole of society. The faith in the Mother of God was really active among men; it penetrated from end to end that great awakening of the spiritual life of the Church which began about the time of St. Bernard, one of the greatest champions of devotion and love of the Mother of God. His call roused the knighthood of Europe to defend the honor of Christ, and he it was who, at the same time, reestablished the great houses of prayer, and gave new life to the monastic institutions through his reform of the Benedictine Order. There, in those houses of prayer, the Virgin's figure and influence brought back again the purity and chaste charity of the primitive Church. The figure of the Virgin, as we may witness in the ruins of a great civilization, stood in every public place and enriched the houses of the poor.

The influence of Mary is not one of feverish stimulation; it is not some public enthusiasm and inconstant fashion of an age. True, in some ages there has been greater devotion to the Mother of God than in others; but it has never been lacking in the hearts of the faithful. It comes from the appreciation of a person who is very close to God. Mary's influence and renown have nothing in common with that popularity which waxes and wanes from age to age, now fervent, now cold. She enters the hearts of the faithful as if each alone was in need of her regard and care. Devotion to the Mother of God is, in the truest sense, a personal devotion. Other Saints have power of influencing us in a certain way. Thus, they become the patrons and patronesses of certain types of people engaged in the same state of life. These Saints attract and encourage the faithful in a certain direction, perhaps to the contemplative life, perhaps to active works of charity. Our Lady is universally renowned, because, in our regard, her influence is one with the Holy Spirit of God.

The Holy Spirit, by the gifts and graces we have considered, has called us to sanctify ourselves in some particular state of life, whether in the cloister or in the world. Our devotion to the Mother of God will be determined by this vocation to which we are called; by this we mean that Mary, knowing what is the will of the Holy Spirit in our regard, will show herself to us in that special light which will the more readily fit in with the purposes of the Holy Ghost. She has for this reason become the "Queen of Confessors," because she knew, more than any other, what discipleship with the Divine Son must mean; she had been the Mother of the first disciples of her Son and their chief comfort when He had left them. She has become the "Queen of Virgins," for she claimed nothing more than that she might at all times be the Handmaid of the Lord.

In the Middle Ages, Mary gave to the faithful the gift of her Holy Rosary. By this means she placed in the hands of all an instrument of prayer and contemplation, which for the faithful may be compared to the Divine Office of the Church. Not only in the contemplative life did she draw men to sanctity, but equally exerted her power in the growing activity of the following ages.

Men raise monuments to and record in art and literature that only which most directly influences their lives, furthers their happiness, and stimulates their ideals. In every department of self and civic expression men have honored the Virgin Queen, second only to her Son. Her churches cover many lands; her shrines draw saints and sinners from far and near, and there she encourages the one and heals the other. Even after the dire effects of the Reformation, the art and literature of the past show how intimate, how real, was the influence of Mary on the hearts of the faithful.

The Holy Virgin has not only drawn men to herself. She has sent forth sons and daughters to preach and to teach, to heal body and soul by her aid. And so, while having a tender regard for our needs and ills, she has gained for herself the esteem and honor, the gratitude and love, of men and women living in the most remote corners of the world. Wherever we hear the rattle of the Rosary beads of some friar or nun, we know that the Mother of God is sending one of her disciples to bring cheer and charity in her name. Blessed, indeed, art thou among women!

## XXXVIII

# The Voice of the People

*Her children rose up, and called her Blessed (Prov., xxxi. 28).*

In the preceding consideration we suggested that prayer is a revelation of the spirit, a manifestation of the inner thoughts and desires of mankind, concerning man's attitude towards God and his honor of those who have come close to the friendship of God. If we take one of the chief prayers given us by Catholic tradition and consider it in some detail, we shall see how true this is.

Let us suppose, once again, that a complete stranger comes across the litany of the Mother of God, hidden away in some forgotten book, when all that was once a Christian civilization had passed away in our Western world. What would such a stranger find, what would this prayer reveal to him?

He would note the attitude of humble approach

of the soul in a prayer which, though dedicated to the Blessed Virgin, turns first in contrition to God who is Three in One. This threefold invocation of mercy is addressed to the Father, Son and Holy Ghost, from whom we have received all things, through whom we have been redeemed, and by whom we have been sanctified. Such a prayer is one of faith. It is only by grace that we can conceive and accept a mystery so deep as this: it is essentially a Christian prayer. It speaks of Fatherhood, Sonship and Love, each Divine, each Divinely Personified, yet united in one nature of the Godhead —the Source of Divine Mercy. We ask mercy of the Father, for who would understand our need more than He who sent His only Begotten Son into the world? We ask mercy of the Son, for He won us back to the kingdom of light when we were in darkness. We ask mercy of the Spirit of Love, for He has sanctified us in truth.

By the same deep faith, we turn, then, to the Word made flesh, with that invocation so often addressed to Him on earth: "Christ, hear us, Christ, graciously hear us." Like the poor of old we cry: "Jesus, Son of David, have mercy on us."

Then, from the Son we turn to the Mother; for we remember that with His dying breath He gave her to us as *our* Mother. But this time we ask her to make our petition her own: "Pray for us."

After showing forth our faith, our prayer is then turned towards Mary herself, and this is a prayer of petition that she would pray for us. Again, a stranger would see how Mary stands at the foot of the throne of God, in the form and figure of an advocate for the children of men. In this first phase of our prayer, directed immediately to Mary, we give her three titles of great dignity, titles which show how much greater than any other creature she is in our eyes, and by the privilege of divine grace: Holy Mary, Holy Mother of God, Holy Virgin of virgins! It was the Archangel of God who gave her the first title: Holy, full of grace. It was God, who gave to her the singular honor of being the Mother of the Son of God, and, at the same time of remaining a virgin.

In the next phase of our prayer, we turn to this Holy Virgin as Mother. Her Motherhood is two-fold; she was truly the Mother of Christ, our Savior, and, as He was the Word of God, she is also the

222

Mother of our Creator. Our prayer, therefore, is directed to one whose Son holds the power of the natural world and the world of grace, of salvation and redemption, in His hands; the Mother of Divine Grace! What is there in this world or in the next that He does not possess? Whatever needs we have, whether of this world or the world of grace, she has but to ask of Him, and He will grant it to her.

Mary's Motherhood also has reference to our rebirth in the sanctifying grace of the Holy Spirit of God. She is the Mother of Divine Grace in so far as she gave to the world the Source of all grace. That the Holy Spirit may dwell by grace within us, it is necessary that we be pure and chaste of soul and body; this is why we appeal, in our prayer, to the Mother most chaste and pure among women, to the Mother most admirable and amiable.

The third phase of our prayer appeals to the Holy Virgin, and here we give her those titles which seem most fitting to her because of the evidence of her character, as found in the Sacred Scripture. These titles are inspired by the picture given us by the word of God, directed by the Holy Spirit. We, who are in such need of the graces which we find in the Mother of God, appeal to her as the Virgin most prudent, faithful, powerful and merciful; and, because she has helped so many towards a life of grace, we address her as the Virgin most venerable and renowned.

The next titles with which we address the Mother of God would have little meaning to a stranger to our faith, but to us they are most intimate acknowledgments of what she means to us. We have seen how much is meant by the title "Mirror of Justice," but those of "Seat of Wisdom" and "Cause of our Joy" immediately make us think of her as the means which God chose to give to the world that wisdom which can alone bring peace and happiness to mankind. The term used in the next three titles is "Vessel," referring to the Immaculate soul of Mary in which the Holy Spirit was enshrined. The last of these titles is directed to Mary who has taken such an intimate care in our every-day affairs.

"Mary, Help of Christians," how rich in memories this title is for Christian men and women! We think of Mary who inspired the Founders of the Orders who rescued the Christians by ransom-money, and their own lives at times, to save the slaves from Mohammedan prisons; we think of the time when this title was a battle-cry for those defending the West from the invasion of the Turks; we recall this title was a battle-cry for those defending the great modern apostle, St. John Bosco, who saved the souls of the young from the paganism of today.

"Comfort of the Afflicted," "Health of the Sick," here each human soul bears witness to its own great need. But, perhaps, we associate these titles most naturally with those great pilgrimages of old and modern times to the shrines of the Mother of God, where she has, so to speak, stooped down to us to give evidence of her solicitude for the afflicted and suffering, by a more visible and motherly presence, by her acts of miraculous curing at Lourdes, Fatima, and Guadaloupe.

"Refuge of Sinners." Who shall number the men and women who have called upon Mary under this title and have consequently found the courage to rise up and go to their Father and say, "I have sinned against heaven, and against Thee," and have received the peace and security of the grace of a good confession? Though we strike our breasts with the consciousness of sin when making this prayer, it is with new faith and a new hope that we invoke her under this title, for we know that she has but to ask her Son, as she did at Cana, and we will receive the wine of His Divine Mercy.

Though royalties have disappeared from most countries in the world to-day, we think it no incongruity to give the title of "Queen" to Mary, because, as she rules over our own hearts, we know that she has ruled over all those who have shared in the reign of Christ. Thus we address her as "Queen of All Saints," knowing that she has first place in the Heavenly Court.

We close this prayer with a petition to the Lamb of God, who taketh away the sins of the world, once again to have mercy on us, who have put our faith in the prayers of His Holy Mother.

This traditional prayer to the Mother of our Savior is an index, showing us the historical devotion of the faithful, and the continued efficacy of the Motherhood of Mary in the lives of those children whom she received at the foot of the Cross. To read this prayer is to read a great deal of the history of the Mystical Body of Christ.

# Epilogue

We began these considerations with a reference to Cardinal Newman's *Second Spring*, and we can do no better than close them with his words, a prayer to the Virgin Mother. We must feel the inadequacy of any real and solid virtue, unless there is the Holy Spirit of God abiding with us, for the Spirit has given us this warning: "Unless the Lord build the house, they labor in vain that build it. Unless the Lord keep the city, he watcheth in vain that keepeth it" (Ps., cxxvi. 1).

If, then, there is to be a revival of the spiritual values in the world to-day, whether individually or corporately, it will be because the Holy Spirit of God has inspired us to know, love and serve Him more faithfully. This inspiration may well come to us through the contemplation of the Virgin, whom He made His Spouse, so that the Incarnate Word might dwell with us, and that He should abide with us all days even to the consummation of the world.

We close these pages with a deep feeling of hope,

and the foundation of this hope is not so much in the things that have happened in the past, but rather in the dim light of another dawn, a light breaking around the figure of Mary, the Morning Star.

Though men have done their uttermost to undermine the Christian way of life, though they have through their various agencies tried to defile that way of life with widespread paganism, they have only succeeded in part. Into the darkness of a materialistic age there has come the light of the apparitions of the Immaculate Virgin. Where men have tried to dethrone the image of the Virgin, it is there that she has appeared in a form and manner they could not touch, certainly in a manner they could not explain. Within the lifetime of most of us, she has appeared again to little children, giving them her message to the world. It is as if she intended to begin her reign among men all over again.

The Image of Our Lady of Fatima has been carried in triumph through the villages, towns and cities of many nations, bringing to them a new hope in the strength and purpose of her visitation among men. The way she has travelled has been blessed by the conversion of the greatest enemies of spirituality, of men and women hardened in the principles of materialism, of men and women defiled with the contagions of an impure culture, if culture it may be called. Her Immaculate Heart has drawn men and women to repentance, turning them back to the things they loved and valued in their childhood, but which they lost in the lust for riches and for pleasure.

We, thanks be to God, are witnessing something of the new stirrings of spiritual life which were seen in the days of St. Bernard, in the age of Dominic, Francis and Anthony; something new to us of to-day, but as old as the Church itself. The Virgin has taken a new form, but her purpose and her compassion for men are the same—her purpose is to renew the face of the earth, to crush the heel of the enemy of mankind; her compassion urges her to come again to the aid of men, when a new shadow of darkness is passing over the face of humanity. She has promised us, as she promised St. Pius V, that we shall conquer, if we but turn to her.

These pages, like her many statues, reflect now

one, now another of her many attributes and virtues. But they are only meant to make men pause,
to think, to pray, to come closer to her, to embrace
the hand she extends to them. Some will be attracted by this phase of her spiritual life, some by
that. Some will find one reflection more helpful
than another; let them linger there as long as they
will. How great is the plenitude of the grace of
Mary! How varied her life with God! One is re-
minded of the words of Gilbert K. Chesterton, one
of her greatest modern poets. He is recalling this
universal love of men for the Mother of God, and
how they have tried to depict her in her many attributes. He was thinking of one unique statue of
hers; we are thinking of that latest expression of
her love for men: Our Lady of Fatima. Would he
not use these words of his again, if he were with
us now?

"One in thy thousand statues we salute thee
    On all thy thousand thrones acclaim and
        claim
    Who walk in forest of thy forms and faces
    Walk in a forest calling on one name.
    . . . I have found thee like a little shepherdess

Gay in green ribbons; and passed on to find
Michael, called Angel, hew the Mother of God
Like one that fills a mountain with a mind:
Molten in silver or gold or garbed in blue,
Or garbed in red where the inner robe burns
    through,
Of the King's daughter glorious within:
Change thine unchanging light with every
    hue,
Clothed with the sun or standing on the
    moon
Crowned with the stars or single, a Morning
    Star." *

These pages are an incomplete record of Mary, the Spouse of the Holy Ghost; it is to be hoped that they may do a little to further devotion to her Immaculate Heart, that a New Spring may refresh the earth. Such is the prayer of Cardinal Newman:

"Arise, Mother of God, and with thy thrilling voice speak to those who labor with child, and are in pain, till the babe of grace leaps within

---

* "The Black Virgin" (from "Queen of the Seven Swords," Sheed & Ward, 1944).

them! Shine on us, dear Lady, with thy bright countenance, like the sun in his strength, O *Stella Matutina*, O Harbinger of peace, till our year is one perpetual May. From thy sweet eyes, from thy pure smile, from thy majestic brow, let ten thousand influences rain down, not to confound or overwhelm, but to persuade, to win over thine enemies. O Mary, my hope, O Mother undefiled, fulfill to us the promise of this Spring."